BUILDING BLOCKS OF THE MIND

A Powerful Protocol For Clearing Mental Distress

Peter Owen

PSTEC Master Practitioner

For a personal consultation visit: www.themindhealer.co.uk

Published by Lulu Enterprises Inc.
3101 Hillsborough Street
Suite 210
Raleigh, NC 27607-5436
United States of America

Published in paperback 2018
Category: Reference
Copyright Peter Owen © 2018
ISBN : 978-0-244-10430-6

For a personal consultation visit: www.themindhealer.co.uk

Note from the Author

This book describes a multitude of therapeutic techniques and ideas. One key method is the use of Percussive Suggestion Technique (PSTEC).

Most readers will arrive at this book through PSTEC but for those who haven't, it is a powerful set of audio tools which needs to be purchased separately.

For a personal consultation visit: www.themindhealer.co.uk

Table of Contents

For a personal consultation visit: www.themindhealer.co.uk

Foreword

There are ways of doing therapy which could quite frequently leave other therapists scratching their heads as they try to figure out exactly how it was made to look so easy. If you read Peter's work carefully then it will utterly change the way you do everything.

The ideal in therapy is to have a system which can be universally applied. One wants a method which works time and time again. Even better is to have a way of working which will solve problems that no one else could solve before.

Such a method is pretty much what you're holding in your hands right now. It probably sounds like it should be complicated to learn. Well... that rather depends on the method, the system, and the teacher. It also depends upon the world view that you take.

Amongst other things Peter has written extensively here about PSTEC(TM) which is a methodology and also suite of therapy tools which I created. Through multiple tutorials I've taught people how to use PSTEC for all manner of problems, but as

For a personal consultation visit: www.themindhealer.co.uk

they say, "two heads are often better than one" and some therapists go far beyond what they've ever been taught.

Peter's mastery of PSTEC has been simply extraordinary and he certainly hasn't stopped there. Instead of just mastering what's in my own tutorials Peter has become a kind of therapy ninja. He's gone beyond any tutorials from any source and he has developed his own unique methods.

He's fused PSTEC with other things and with brilliant strategies of his own devising. The results have been truly spectacular. Some therapists would keep such skills to themselves preferring to have "an edge" or jealously guarding their secrets. Instead it's with real generosity that Peter has taken the time to carefully explain what he's done so that others can do the same. There's lots here that I wish I'd thought of myself. I thank him immensely.

Albert Einstein is reputed to have said, that if you cannot explain something simply, then you do not understand it. Ask most doctors how to cure most mental health or behavioural problems and you'll never get a straight answer. They can't explain because they simply don't know.

By contrast the world's greatest therapists often do know but seldom get the attention they deserve. Occasionally a great therapist is also a great teacher. That is the ideal. The world's greatest teachers understand their subject so thoroughly that they can also teach it, and great teachers can explain even the most complex aspects in beautifully simple ways.

For a personal consultation visit: www.themindhealer.co.uk

Fortunately Peter is one such person and he will take you step by step through all that you need to know in order to utterly transform your therapy abilities. You'll also learn much more along the way.

If you follow these methods you will frequently appear to work miracles, but they are not miracles. One person's "miracle" is simply the predictable outcome of doing certain things in certain ways. Peter has taken powerful tools that work well already and he has carefully and brilliantly refined their application in a truly beautiful way.

My personal advice is to dip into the middle of the book first and start by reading a few case histories. Doing that will give you a clue as to the simplicity and sheer power of what you're about to learn. Then I suggest to go back to page one and read through to from start to finish. Peter will lay it out for you step by step and he will illustrate with countless examples. It's an honour and a privilege to have been asked to write a foreword to this remarkable book.

This book is a practical encapsulation of years of work, much of it that Peter has done working with extremely troubled youngsters. Many of these young people had been totally failed by existing or traditional methods. Using these new methods the problems have been solved time and again, often both quickly and easily. By the time you finish reading you'll know exactly how.

As well as introducing this book I would also like to thank Peter

For a personal consultation visit: www.themindhealer.co.uk

for his support, kindness and friendship. Knowing him is a perpetual joy. We met as strangers though a shared interest in this kind of work but along the way we have found that we also share many other interests and attitudes.

Rather than ramble on I will simply thank Peter for writing such a brilliant work.

Tim Phizackerley
Creator of PSTEC(TM)

Introduction

I am passionate about helping those who are suffering from mental distress. Having previously suffered from anxiety myself I know how bad things can get, which has driven me to research and experiment in an attempt to bring people to peace and calm as quickly as possible. Like many therapists I have found value in cognitive approaches which identify the thinking which is playing a role and challenging problematic beliefs. I have found value in researching other modalities also. In any area of interest I find myself, I have a need to constantly experiment, refine, add bits in and take bits out and observe the change. This has included adding other modalities into the mix and playing around with different ways of applying them.

Since my previous two therapy books I am in an interesting position. Working in schools, I have had many 100's of children to work with. The school setting allows me to get long-term information and follow-up from them both pupils and staff, and as such it provides the perfect feedback mechanism. In that time I've also received many requests to more fully explain what I am doing to get the results I have been obtaining, and now seems a good time to do so.

For a personal consultation visit: www.themindhealer.co.uk

This is a book of case studies that outlines both my approach and how it can be applied in many areas. Some of it will be familiar to all those in the helping professions: understanding someone's world, developing of a therapeutic relationship, challenging patterns of thoughts and belief, etc. Some of it will be new to many, like the tools I use such as Percussive Suggestion Technique (PSTEC) audio tracks, which I believe can deal with certain problems that seem to respond to little else.

This is not a book on theory. Ultimately, what interests me most is what works, and how to replicate that success as many times and with as little trouble as possible. Due to the nature of working in schools, I have developed an approach which aims to work rapidly and requires little effort on behalf of the client. In this work you will hear of a traumatised lady whose appearance visibly changed dramatically before her very eyes following the deconstruction of a belief. You will hear about a boy who heard voices which made predictions which always seemed to come true. You will learn about how a long term school refuser suddenly started going to school simply by using a different word for school; and more importantly, why this worked. Within and among these examples, I will try to distil my 1000's of trial and error into something that provides the reader with a window into my framework and my results, whether to satisfy curiosity or to inform their own practice.

I shall begin with outlining a simple framework through which I work with pretty much anyone and any problem. This will include outlining some useful philosophical perspectives to consider when helping clients or for self-helpers which I find

For a personal consultation visit: www.themindhealer.co.uk

extremely powerful and a great way to get clients in the right mind-set for this kind of work. Although, initially, this might not seem that important from a practical perspective, it is perhaps one of the more crucial aspects in that it allows what follows to work with the least amount of resistance possible.

Of particular interest to psychologists and cognitive behaviour therapists will be the role that challenging beliefs plays within the framework. It will be shown that often entire structures of disempowering thoughts can be wiped away through a quick process of emotional clearing at the start of a session and sometimes this is all that is required for lasting change. Any that remain can be identified and challenged as part of the therapy and often be met with less resistance.

Psychologists who work with clients will doubtless be aware of the fact that once a person can see rationally that certain ideas and beliefs are false or unhelpful, it is quite common for the person to still "feel" as though the old thinking is correct. Rather than just challenging those beliefs, the techniques described within show how to make the new ways of thinking much more robust, all-encompassing and actually "feel" real, often without any ongoing work on behalf of either the client or therapist.

There will be some theory but there will be a strong focus on the practical application of these principles in the form of case studies. You will see what to do when a particular approach doesn't work in a wide range of settings. What may appear slick is the result of trial and error over many cases, constantly attempting to improve and thinking of new ideas and

For a personal consultation visit: www.themindhealer.co.uk

applications. You will learn processes here which, even a few years ago, may have left me scratching my head when presented with that scenario by a client.

Because each problem is dealt with through the same general framework, you may find that a case study involving anger, may help someone who suffers from an eating disorder or anxiety. Or someone suffering from grief may find something of use in the trauma section. I have included a large proportion of quite severe cases as these are more likely to show all parts of the framework in action than, for example, a simple phobia removal. There are also a much greater number of cases involving children than adults. However, the way it is written should allow for the principles to be drawn from it and applied where needed in your life or practice.

The chapters are quite loosely defined in terms of specific problems or processes to be described. I say loosely because everything really is linked and so there will be some overlap. I hope that whether you are a self-helper or a therapist working with clients, you will find something of interest here that will help you on your journey. This is a work in progress and I suspect I'll have streamlined the process even more over the next few years.

Although PSTEC isn't the sole focus of this book, it does often play a key role in making progress when problems occur. Therefore, before I get to the framework, I think it a good idea to briefly describe the PSTEC audio tracks I'll be referring to. PSTEC provides a great quick way to turn down bad feelings which aren't serving a useful purpose. It also fits hand in glove for those occasions in which through conversation a client can clearly see that certain beliefs are false or aren't working, yet the alternatives just don't seem real to them. For those already familiar with PSTEC this paragraph will serve as a quick reminder. For those new to PSTEC, before moving on I recommend taking a look at Appendix 1 where I give a more thorough explanation of the tracks and what they do. Even for someone brand new to PSTEC, this information should suffice to gain value from this work and to see what is possible.

The PSTEC audio tools are called Click Tracks. There are various kinds of Click Track but these include:

1. Emotion Clearing Click Tracks: This includes the basic Click Tracks, Enhanced Effectiveness Files (EEF) and Click Track 2015.
2. Belief Change Tracks: PSTEC Positive to embed a new belief and PSTEC Negative and Belief Blasters to undo a disempowering belief.
3. Cascade Release: This is a track which can be used when there is no known cause of an emotion.

Throughout the book if I mention use of a Click Track, I am referring to one of the emotion clearing tracks. For others I shall often specify which exact track I'll be using.

* The techniques described translate into all types of therapy environment but professionals reading this who may be considering such uses do need to be aware that corporate type

For a personal consultation visit: www.themindhealer.co.uk

uses of PSTEC are subject to certain restrictions or licensing. For this reason all therapists using PSTEC should carefully read the terms of use.

If you happen to be interested in school type uses it is essential to visit www.healthyyoungminds.co.uk

The Framework

Not all parts of the framework will be utilised each and every time. What is required depends on the unique model of reality the person has, what the problem is and how it developed. Also important is whether the problem is propped up by disempowering beliefs/thinking/emotions, their situation in life and a few other factors which I'll get to shortly.

For more complex problems, often a combination of approaches are required and the path only becomes clear as you move along and analyse the results after each particular piece of action is taken. As I go through the case studies you will see how certain patterns seem to form, such as the use of PSTEC Positive (belief change tool) in a particular way being a key early part of therapy for those who have suffered a trauma which is very recent. In my early "PSTEC" days I may have incorrectly thought that if the powerful emotion neutralisers like the EEF fail to have an impact, then PSTEC Positive isn't likely to have much chance.

By having this framework and set of approaches at the back of your mind, you will be more likely to have additional ideas for

For a personal consultation visit: www.themindhealer.co.uk

moving forward when things get a little tricky or don't go as expected.

The 6 tactics within the framework are:

1. Discussing the philosophical and psychological nature of beliefs and consciousness. This often forms part of the pre-talk and the aim is to make a person very suggestible to new ideas and ways of thinking.
2. Clearing emotions.
3. Identifying, adding, and removing beliefs that either form part of the problem or lead to a solution. This also includes metaphorical and conceptual reframes, massively enhanced through PSTEC Positive and Negative (described below).
4. Identifying what resources a person has and using them as leverage. This includes both internal resources already existing in a person's model of reality as well as external resources.
5. The teaching of new skills.
6. Identifying tasks that can be carried out to solidify the work carried out or actually as the key method for changing that person's model of reality.

On paper the usefulness of these 6 tactics might not be immediately clear but I shall expand on these ideas and, more importantly, breathe life into them via case studies. In the case studies you shall see time and again how the 6 tactics can work together to achieve results where failure might result otherwise.

The Nature of Beliefs, Perception and Experience

When it comes to philosophical and psychological perspectives, I consider their value based on their ability to improve a person's experience of life. In Robert Anton Wilson's excellent book "Quantum Psychology" he writes extensively about the nature of belief and perception. Any particular belief or perception we hold he calls a "reality tunnel" as opposed to reality itself.

He describes an old Chinese fable of a farmer whose coin purse went missing. The farmer was very puzzled and wondered how he could have lost it. He then realised that a local farm boy was the last person who had been to his house and began to suspect he had possibly stolen it. As the days went by he noticed that the boy seemed to be acting quite suspiciously. If he looked at the boy, he would quickly look away with a guilty look on his face.

After a week or so of this the farmer was becoming more and more angry and decided to confront the boy's parents. He headed over and was just about to bang on the door when his wife called out that she had found his purse in their house. He instantly remembered putting it in this other location and marvelled how he could have forgotten.

So what does this fable tell us? It shows how our expectation and beliefs can radically alter our "reality tunnels" and experience in a particular area of life. Was he actually seeing guilty behaviour or simply imagining it? On the surface we would probably assume that he was imagining it but it is also possible that his beliefs

For a personal consultation visit: www.themindhealer.co.uk

were impacting his behaviour which, in turn, was altering how the boy was behaving around him. For example, if every time the boy looks up he sees the farmer glaring at him, it is possible he felt intimidated and therefore looked away.

As I have described elsewhere this is an example of what psychologists describe as confirmation bias. That is, once we form a belief, we have a tendency to interpret further information as backing up the original idea and to dismiss or selectively ignore evidence to the contrary. Only once his wife found his coin purse was that particular "reality tunnel" popped, allowing him to experience a different version of reality.

Beliefs

I wrote quite extensively in PSTEC Advanced Part 2 about the idea that we should treat our beliefs with scepticism; especially those that lead us to pain. Due to limitations of our nervous system, we literally cannot experience reality directly. Our brain has to construct our experience of reality. It does this through sensory inputs which are filtered and analysed through our "model of reality". It could be said that to a large extent we start off with a blank slate which gets added to as we go through life. The different experiences we have as we go through life shape and amend our model of reality in the format of beliefs, memories, emotions and much more. It is through the model of reality that we process the incoming information, at which point

For a personal consultation visit: www.themindhealer.co.uk

our brains present our awareness with one potential portrayal of reality.

In the fable above, the farmer's model of reality gave birth to the idea that the farm boy had possibly stolen the money. This one alteration in his model of reality had a huge impact on the way his brain processed the sensory information about the boy from that point on.

To further illustrate this point, here is an example of one of the first people I ever worked with in a school who had severe anger. By all accounts he was fighting daily and was on the verge of permanent exclusion. He felt he was constantly under attack and his model of reality was providing a great deal of evidence for this in the form of "people looking him the wrong way" and "teachers being unfair". He came into my office and kicked over the desk I was sat behind. I suspected he may have just had a fight but when I asked what had happened, he replied, "Nothing! I'm always like this!". I describe in the appendix how I am able to bypass resistance and gain rapport in a situation like this.

He was 14 at the time and I asked if he felt under so much attack by others when he was 10. He scowled that he had been under attack and therefore angry all of his life. To his growing frustration I continued asking the same question at slightly earlier times in his life until we got to the age of 3 and he admitted that he wasn't angry then and so he assumed mustn't have been under attack at that point. He also conceded and realised that it began at the age of 4, when he endured a trauma that he hadn't thought about for a very long time.

His father had severely beaten both him and his mother as well as smashing their house to pieces. He was shaking with rage at this memory which occurred 10 years ago. He hadn't seen his father since and had no desire to do so. In fact, he thought if he ever saw his father, revenge would be the foremost thought on his mind.

I asked if he would prefer to get rid of this intense anger to which he defiantly said "no chance". I then went on to explain that getting rid of the anger was in no way, shape or form forgiving his father. In fact he could think whatever he liked about his father regardless, but that removing the anger was just like getting rid of a bad headache he had been carrying around for a long time. In a sense, these ways of looking at the situation were themselves altering his model of reality, in that his barriers to removing the anger became much weaker.

He agreed to try out an emotional clearing Click Track and in his case all it took is one listen to remove all of his intense anger. As many people do straight after such a big clearance, he just stared into space, confused yet calm. He told me with a big grin on his face that he doesn't ever remember feeling so calm. I asked him to try to bring back the anger thinking about the event, to which he burst into laughter saying, "I don't get it! I just don't get it!".

I saw him two weeks later and his day to day life experience had changed beyond recognition. All fighting had completely stopped and miraculously, it felt to him that the teachers were being much fairer to him also. In fact, the whole world just seem much kinder to him. So what exactly happened here? Of course

- 24 -

external reality didn't change but in removing the anger from the past trauma, not only had a lot of steam been let out of his system but also the belief that he was "under attack" seemed to have evaporated also. This is despite the fact that no direct work on that belief had been carried out.

This slight modification in his model of reality completely altered the experience of life that his brain was creating for him. It was probably a combination of him interpreting certain scenarios more leniently and also people responding to him different due to him feeling calmer. The power to make this kind of change to your model of reality is extremely powerful.

What can we take away from this? Through the work of ancient eastern philosophers and the more open minded present day psychologists, therapists and philosophers, a very powerful and useful way of looking at beliefs can be ascertained:

Beliefs are not reality. They are a vague approximation of what "might be out there". Because beliefs are a mere approximation of reality it could be said that in a way, whilst there may be some truth to certain beliefs, by definition all beliefs are at least partially wrong. Therefore the truth or falsehood of belief is less important than we might otherwise think. What is important is whether the belief allows us to function in the world and whether it leads us to peace and happiness or stress and worry.

This mindset is both important and useful. It paves the way for implanting new beliefs and removing old beliefs in way that is met with the least resistance by a person's existing model of

For a personal consultation visit: www.themindhealer.co.uk

reality. It works at a deeper level than typical cognitive strategies which operate more at the level of what beliefs and thinking are present, rather than thinking about the illusory nature of beliefs as a whole. It is a key underpinning reframe which can make new perspectives much easier to take on-board, whatever the presenting issue.

The Model of Reality Revisited

From my experience and research, if there are big emotions involved, it is often best to clear these with the Click Tracks as a first port of call (Basic Click Tracks, EEF's, Click Track Accelerators, Click Track 2015) rather than challenge the thinking that comes with them. The reason for this is that doing so often automatically clears problem beliefs and can have a huge impact on person's experience of reality. If a big emotion struggles to be cleared with Click Tracks, this suggests a more cognitive and belief orientated solution might be more beneficial. Overall I have found that clearing emotions prior to working at the belief level to be the most efficient and easiest way of making progress.

Think of the model of reality as a meaning making system whose job it is to protect you. Obviously via the pleasure/pain principle and emotions, it guides us towards some things and away from others. It also holds all of our 1000's of beliefs. In the previous example the boy who had been beaten by his father held beliefs such as "I am under attack" or "people are dangerous". Beliefs of

For a personal consultation visit: www.themindhealer.co.uk

this nature would likely result in anger for survival reasons; after all if in danger from aggressors, anger makes perfect sense as you will be better equipped to fight people off. At the opposite end of the spectrum may be beliefs like "I can achieve anything I set out to achieve" which would likely leave a person feeling confident and lead them to take action in scenarios where they may not have done so without it.

Concepts

The following information may lose those who aren't already familiar with this field of knowledge. If this includes you, please read on anyway because all will become clear as you progress. One of the smallest particles within a model of reality is a concept. Although philosophers have debated over 1000's of years what a concept is, for the sake of convenience, let's stick to this working definition: a concept is an abstract mental representation of something.

Concepts can be used to denote concrete objects such as a "table". Within a person's model of reality the concept of table is likely to contain a list of attributes such as legs, horizontal flat surface, designed to support smaller objects, whilst omitting specifics such as how tall the legs are and what material they are made of. In other words it separates items that match these specifications from the rest of sensory experience and thought, and categorizes them as one unit.

For a personal consultation visit: www.themindhealer.co.uk

Other concepts exist at a higher level of abstraction, relying on lower level perceptual concepts to give them meaning. For example consider the concept of "motion". A child can perceive motion but in order to conceptualise it within his model of reality he must have already conceptualised entities/objects that can move, otherwise the concept of motion would be meaningless. The aforementioned example of "table" could be sat within the concept of "furniture" which is another layer of abstraction up and could be defined as containing a number of entities which are movable and allow a particular building or room suitable for working or living in.

So what has all of this got to do with helping clients or improving our own experience of reality? All words are symbols denoting a concept. On the surface it appears as though the words we use are quite standard and when one person says, for example, the word "alone", we suspect that it means the same thing to us. However, especially at these higher levels of abstraction, words and concepts can actually mean very different things to different people. It all depends how it is constructed in their model of reality. Moreover, it is important to note that concepts aren't reality themselves but rather a map of reality that we use to navigate through the world.

The term "the map is not the territory" was first coined by Albert Korzybski in his 1933 book, "Science and Sanity: An Introduction to Non-Aristotelian Systems and General Semantics". It perfectly describes the relationship of our concepts and beliefs to reality and our habit of mistaking our roadmap for the road itself. As you shall see as we go through this book, being consciously aware of this fact gives us much

For a personal consultation visit: www.themindhealer.co.uk

freedom in engineering our experience of the terrain simply by amending our "map". It also allows us to exploit this tendency to get a better idea of where specific problems lie within our own map. The PSTEC suite of tools in combination with cognitive strategies, in essence allows us to become God-like map makers and therefore shape our reality to a large extent.

In a therapy or self-help setting it is important to be on the lookout for certain "problem" concepts. These are often emotionally charged ideas which often crop up by the repeated use of a word such as "alone" or "unfairness". As mentioned before, whether a particular concept such as "alone" is emotionally charged for any particular person depends on how it is constructed within their model of reality. One person might feel quite content spending months alone and may actually feel free. Another person might feel completely alone despite being surrounded by loved ones. In other words there isn't an inherent problem with any particular concept but rather how it is constructed within a person's mind.

In this piece of work you will see many practical examples of how modifying even just one particular concept in a person's model of reality through conversation, can change everything for them. You will also see many examples of how a single concept can be de-charged or restructured, through conversation and sometimes through the PSTEC suite of tools to achieve a similar result.

For a personal consultation visit: www.themindhealer.co.uk

The Critical Faculty

In this section I shall be talking about various ideas to bear in mind when working with yourself or others, in terms of getting past the critical faculty with the least amount of resistance before any tracks have been played. For any change to be made to the model of reality and therefore our experience of life, it must first get past the critical faculty. Think of the critical faculty as a gatekeeper which analyses incoming information and by using logic and past experience, it will decide whether to accept or reject the new information from entering our model of reality. Tim Phizackerley has talked extensively about the critical faculty in PSTEC Advanced so I won't go into too much detail here. However there are a few things I would like to discuss which will make understanding the later chapters in this book easier to understand.

If you are presented with any information which differs to that already contained within your model of reality, whether it bypasses the gatekeeper or not depends on whether the new information has an impact on your safety and survival. Actual safety and survival are less important than whether your model of reality perceives a situation to be dangerous. If it is viewed as neutral from a survival perspective, the acceptance or rejection of the new information is likely to be carried out largely through the process of logic and referencing past experiences, with no emotions involved.

For a personal consultation visit: www.themindhealer.co.uk

However when the new information has the potential to make a change which would impact a survival emotion such as anxiety or anger, it makes sense that the gatekeeper is more cautious. Accepting the wrong piece of information could literally mean the difference between life or death. Herein lies the problem; although this is a useful facet of our minds, our model of reality can all too often come to the wrong conclusions (especially early in life), or may come to a correct conclusion but not update over time to reflect new circumstances. In the example given earlier of the 4 year old boy who was beaten by his father, it makes complete sense for such an extreme early experience to generate certain emotions and beliefs which may actually serve a useful purpose at that point in time.

Time and again I have observed a lifetime of anxiety, anger or upset caused by a random event or even a misunderstanding which may have occurred in early childhood. Even when a person becomes aware of how things came to be as they are, very often the problem remains as the gatekeeper is reluctant to allow changes to be made.

Expanding the Gatekeeper Metaphor

In his book "The Ellipsis Manual: Analysis and Engineering of Human Behaviour", Chase Hughes provides a nice metaphor which expands on this idea of a gatekeeper. I only came across this very recently and although it hasn't played a direct role in my work, it fits in with my thinking and so it is worth noting here.

He suggests thinking of our subconscious minds (or model of reality) as a medieval castle. Chase goes into more detail than I shall describe here but in the castle are guards, villagers, a king and many different rooms and floors.

The guards at the front of the castle represent the critical faculty as described above. As you approach the castle you can see only what has been designed for you to see. In a sense this is the social "mask" that each of us wears to present an image to the public. Their job is to screen incoming people, information, ideas and experiences and they choose who or what gets through into the castle.

Once you get past the guards you will notice many villagers wandering about the castle. The villagers are friendly but if they spot anything suspicious or begin to doubt your intentions, they will quickly eject you from the castle. The king of the castle represents all of the fears, insecurities and desires of the person, which in turn influences the behaviour of all of the villagers and guards. There are also file assistants whose job it is to take information to the king. However they tend to only bring information which agrees with viewpoints the king already has.

The PSTEC suite of tools, due to how they have been constructed, are very effective at getting past the guards, entering the castle and making changes that will be beneficial. In a way, running a PSTEC track is a bit like starting a firework display high above the castle. The king and all of the guards and villagers are looking up to observe the display whilst many changes are being made via the language and other features being used on the tracks. In a sense the PSTEC tracks are firing a barrage of new and useful concepts in the form of words and suggestions, directly at a problem area in the model of reality to make changes needed.

Think back to the boy who was carrying around some intense anger and distrust with him when he first entered my office, yet within minutes I had him in the palm of my hand in a state of high rapport. I certainly wasn't particularly nice to him or try to make him comfortable, at least not in a conventional way that most people might respond well to. In fact I am pretty certain if I had taken that approach he probably would have walked out of my office within minutes, which is exactly what the staff expected him to do. Many of the children I work with have already seen numerous mental health professionals and have often had enough. Therefore it is important that I distinguish myself from anyone else they have seen.

For now, just be aware that holding these ideas in mind allows me to perform a sort of mental dance with the client, winning over the hearts and minds of their "castle" before they have told me a thing or done any therapeutic work at all. This is a very powerful position to be in, regardless of what problem is being faced.

As the session progresses it is important to set up their perception of the experience in a way that reduces the risk that they inadvertently undo the good work already done. Although my expectation in most instances is that the change will likely last, just in case some of it comes back, I ask them to think of our work as

For a personal consultation visit: www.themindhealer.co.uk

a series of experiments. After each piece of work we need to let the dust settle and only in a few days or more will we know the outcome. I give a strong indication that success is likely but also give some other possibilities along with what we would do in those scenarios. This puts them in a frame of mind that will more likely lead them to continue with the work and do what needs to be done if required. Without doing this it is too easy for them to dismiss change that isn't 100% and consequently undo it.

It is also useful to discuss with them how they would actually know that they were moving forward in the right direction. For example, if someone was fearful of giving a presentation, I would encourage them to view any reduction in anxiety as a success and movement in the right direction. This still leaves the expectation of massive change but with some damage limitation if 100% success isn't achieved immediately.

Another powerful mindset I seek to encourage is that of the two of us exploring what is currently in their model of reality. For self-helpers, view yourself as an explorer trying to find out what is in there and what may be changed to enhance your experience of life. When working with clients it almost becomes like the two of us in deep rapport trying to solve a puzzle that doesn't really involve either of us, it merely involves a computer that the client possesses (in other words their model of reality).

I use actual stories from my work with other clients to show how we really are at the mercy of our life experiences and how even just one misunderstanding early on in life can completely alter our entire life experience.

- 34 -

It is common for people to completely dismiss events which occurred early in life. Even teenagers often dismiss events which occurred in primary school or earlier, so it goes without saying that adults are even more likely to be victims of this. Here is a true story I often tell to encourage clients never to dismiss any events from the past. I strongly encourage them to view the strength of emotion linked to an event as a much better indicator of importance than when an event occurred or how traumatic it is on paper.

The true story I tell is this:

I once helped a 74 year old lady who came to me after suffering a lifetime of severe anxiety and depression. She believed she had suffered from this since birth and couldn't ever remember not feeling worthless and in danger. She had actually had years of counselling, psychotherapy and psychiatry but nothing seemed to be budging the constant pain she was in.

We began to slowly go back in time through conversation, to different periods of time in her life and different setbacks she had had. Like many people of that age, she had lost loved ones, experienced romantic breakups, lost and gained work etc. There were definite pockets of emotion there but as we approached early childhood in this timeline task, she burst into tears and was inconsolable for a few minutes. At the same time as crying she was berating herself as she couldn't understand why she was so upset over this 70 year old memory which had just surfaced, because on paper it seemed so inconsequential.

For a personal consultation visit: www.themindhealer.co.uk

However this so called "inconsequential event" at the age of 4, which was a mere misunderstanding with her mother was perhaps the most consequential event of her entire life. When she had composed herself she told me what had happened. She had been fighting with her sister when her mother stormed into the room and told her that unless she started behaving, she could pack her bags and leave.

To be clear, I am sure 10 000's of stressed out parents say similar things every day across the world with no real impact on the child (unless the child really is neglected and emotionally abused on a regular basis). As a 74 year old thinking back she also knew that her mother didn't mean it.

However as an impressionable 4 yr old with a model of reality open to any incoming suggestions, her brain accepted this as a real threat. Consequently the essence of these three beliefs sprang into existence within her model of reality.

1. My mother mustn't love me anymore.
2. If my own mother doesn't love me I must be worthless.
3. I might have to look after myself from now on. I can't do this so I am in great danger.

Any child who truly has beliefs such as these is likely to suffer enormously and feel a lot of anxiety. Over the next few years of childhood, other mildly painful events occurred for the lady. However if these other events had occurred in isolation, they very likely would have been dealt with and fizzled away of their own accord. Because they were sat upon a trio of "bad" core beliefs and strong emotions, they got a foothold and the

- 36 -

background feelings grew in power. It's almost like a platform of low self-worth and anxiety had been constructed.

The lady had been through a lot in her life and although pockets of emotion did bubble up when she described some of the other events, the intensity of emotion was nothing compared to the memory of this particular misunderstanding. This was her model of reality indirectly indicating a key problem area.

All it took is one Click Track to remove all emotion from this old memory. However the Click Track did so much more. It completely cleared her anxiety and depression without any further work needing to be done. She wrote to me months later saying that she felt like she had been reborn.

This type of result will be seen often by therapists who utilise PSTEC and work with lots of clients. Most of the case studies I describe in this work will be far more complex and less straightforward than this. However the purpose of describing a story like this to clients is three-fold.

1. It makes them realise how quickly change can occur. However I do make it clear that often a little more work is required, lest they create an impractical success/failure barometer in their mind.
2. It shows that events very early in their life can have a profound impact. This reduces the chance that they will dismiss potential important and emotive events from the past.

3. That our models of reality massively shape our experience of life. It encourages the idea that we aren't trying to change who they are as a person, but tinkering with parts of their model of reality which "aren't working" optimally.

Another indirect and important consequence of this story is the idea that there are different "parts" of us, each with competing viewpoints. The lady had her logical, rational viewpoint which knew that her mother had no intention of kicking her out onto the streets and that she was probably just very stressed, saying it in the heat of the moment.

However another part of her prior to the Click Track, was still seeing it from the perspective of a 4 year old who feels unloved and in danger. I explained that when we have competing viewpoints like this, we can choose which viewpoint would be most useful and once decided, through techniques such as PSTEC we can actually let go of one or the other. Knowing that they have the choice helps keep the king, villagers and guards all onside and open to moving forward.

This story is a great way to temporarily dissociate a person from their model of reality and get them in the best frame of mind possible for change. Many people have a fear of changing who they are and with a story like this, I explain that the lady I helped wasn't at her essence an anxious and depressed person; rather she had an unfortunate early life experience and the real her was sat beneath all of the pain, and then re-emerged once the

For a personal consultation visit: www.themindhealer.co.uk

emotion was cleared. This perspective helps further to keep any potential resistance at bay.

A key takeaway from this and any other story I tell is that an incident has occurred which is often buried deep within memory, yet has a profound impact on a person's thinking, emotions, behaviour, choices etc.

The aim is to bypass as much as possible any potential conscious or subconscious resistance a person has to healing and change. I really do believe that we are all extremely similar and that whilst genetics and nature will play a role, a far greater role is played by the random factors and life experiences that we go through. For example the 74 year old lady had no control over how that particular experience entered her model of reality.

I often tell my clients that if I had their life experiences I very likely would be thinking, feeling and acting as they currently do. Similarly they would likely to be very similar to me if they had my life experiences. In a way, we could say that we are just different versions of the same person, with the variances coming from our differing life experiences and physical appearance.

These kinds of ideas allows them to take a bird's eye view of their model of reality, rendering whatever is happening more of an external problem to be corrected rather than anything inherently wrong with them as a person. It also helps to foster a deep rapport, as not only does it completely take all judgement out of the equation, I truly do believe what I am saying and I think this comes across. When powerful ideas are expressed such

For a personal consultation visit: www.themindhealer.co.uk

as these by someone who lives and breathes them, it seems to have a nourishing impact on the client.

Many people tell me they feel completely at ease with me and feel like they have known me for a long time. I suspect the reason for this is at least in part due to these ideas forming part of my inner script, whether I vocalise them or not. More strikingly, I work with many extremely angry adults and teenagers and I believe I win them over very quickly by conveying these ideas before they even tell me a thing. Self-helpers can benefit massively just by being aware of these kinds of ideas.

One benefit of utilising a technique like PSTEC as part of your arsenal is that great work can be carried out content free. I make it clear to all of my clients that if there are specifics that they would rather not go into, that that is completely fine and we can still achieve great results.

First of all this is true and good for the client to know. Secondly it conveys yet another indirect message that the person's castle/model of reality is completely safe and reduces the risk of any resistance flaring. This is very important, builds up further rapport and often opens up the client further, whether one is using cognitive strategies or otherwise.

Unless a person has experienced something too traumatic to speak about, most of my paying clients are happy to divulge specifics. Children in particular benefit from this knowledge and I often tell give them an example of a child I worked with

For a personal consultation visit: www.themindhealer.co.uk

recently who said that something "bad" had happened last year but hadn't wanted to go into specifics.

I tell them that despite this, I checked if they felt it was safe to let go of the feeling and they did, so we ran the Click Track on the unspecified event and they felt like a massive weight had been lifted and they felt calm about the situation.

Knowing that they don't have to tell me a thing, counter intuitively it often increases the chance that they do tell me what has been going on. I suspect this is because the lack of pressure reduces their resistance enough to feel comfortable talking about it. I also give them the opportunity to write down what has happened, as some people feel more comfortable doing this than saying it aloud, especially for highly emotive events.

Another useful mindset and statement goes along the lines of "I don't care about XYZ; all I care about is you feeling better". This is mostly aimed at school-children as another rapport building statement I often use which discourages a child from seeing me as just another member of staff. For example I may say that I am sure the school would prefer it if you weren't so angry but to be honest I don't really care about the school. And then I say that all I am concerned with is helping you feel calmer and happier.

Again this helps to bypass resistance and help them realise that first and foremost I am on their side which is completely true. This will help them which indirectly will benefit the school. Although much of what I am describing is aimed at bypassing resistance in this chapter, it is also said with sincerity, otherwise

- 41 -

the lack of congruence would be detected by the client thus breaking rapport.

Although much of the time our aim is to bypass resistance to increase the ease with which change occurs, there are some considerations to be aware of. Joergen Rassmusen, author of "Provocative Suggestions" and "Provocative Hypnosis" is a very talented therapist. He studied NLP and Hypnosis and for a while proceeded to treat clients on a no result, no fee basis. This meant that he had to become very effective, very quickly. I also work on this basis with clients but I am fortunate to have PSTEC as part of my repertoire which makes quick change easier than it would otherwise be.

In his work with clients he will often go for a walk and, unbeknown to his client have actors create a scenario which will likely induce change in the client. I love his novel and out of the box thinking. I first came across the notion of a highly hypnotisable client in his "Provocative Suggestions" book where he described the kind of client where you get a seemingly miraculous result, yet shortly after they will come back to your office and the problem will have returned. This group of people seem to be more impacted by any thoughts they have than others may be.

A returning problem doesn't always indicate a highly hypnotisable client but later in the book I shall describe a few case studies which will help therapists identify them. Often they are able to bring up emotions very quickly. These emotions are quick to clear but then the client is easily able to recreate the

For a personal consultation visit: www.themindhealer.co.uk

emotion, even for things which have long since passed with no complicating factors involved. Typically it is best to make the client aware of how impactful their negative self-talk can be and instead, utilise techniques which focus more on the desired outcome.

In terms of their critical faculty and the castle metaphor, it is almost as if their guards, king and villagers will more readily take on-board any incoming input, whether good or bad. In other words it is very easy to get into their castle and make changes. In some ways you could see this as a positive until you realise that the slightest comment by someone else or just a little negative self-talk can be enough to set them back to where they were in the first place.

Most people aren't highly hypnotisable in this sense and often if an emotion or problem comes back, more digging and additional work may be required. Despite this, I thought being aware of this kind of "model of reality" may be useful to have in mind.
Now we have outlined a number of methods to make a person's model of reality as receptive as possible, I shall discuss the usual order in which I work with clients in terms of the dismantling the problem at hand.

Clearing Emotions

In general, no matter what problems a person comes to me with, one of my first aims is to identify key painful emotions and remove them with a PSTEC Click Track. As could be seen in the

For a personal consultation visit: www.themindhealer.co.uk

example of the angry teenage boy and the anxious old lady, clearing emotions made so many other changes beyond what appeared to be occurring on the surface. Entire belief structures contained within the emotion were also dismantled simultaneously and they both had a very different experience of life from that point on, without any further work.

This kind of result is quite normal and is why I almost always begin with removal of painful emotions, even if the event they are linked with seem completely unrelated to the problem at hand.

Beliefs, Concepts and Reframes

Depending on the presenting issue, if clearing an emotion appears to make a huge change I will often follow this up with a PSTEC Positive statement in order to embed or reinforce a useful belief. I have found this to be more effective in creating lasting change, than challenging beliefs and coming up with new beliefs without ramping up the power of them with PSTEC. If any obstacles occur at this point I will do some digging to see if I can determine any problem beliefs hindering process. I will also be on the lookout for problem concepts and either re-shape them conversationally or through a combination of PSTEC Positive and Negative. Sometimes an individual concept can be left as it is but just needs to be de-charged using the emotion clearing Click Tracks. In the same way that a trauma would be cleared, the person would simply think about the problematic

For a personal consultation visit: www.themindhealer.co.uk

idea, bring up the emotional charge and try to keep hold of it whilst going through the track.

On other occasions I will be on the lookout for the perfect PSTEC Positive statement. In fact sometimes the right PSTEC Positive statement will be the only thing that makes the change occur. All of these ideas will be fleshed out with practical examples throughout this book.

Resource Identification

We each possess a huge amount of resources of which there are two broad kinds; internal and external. Internal resources include things like skills, abilities, happy memories, motivation, experience, determination etc. External resources come in the form of things such as our support network, money, work, relationships etc. Although on the surface there appears to be two kinds of resources, all of these resources exist within our model of reality. The external ones are merely how our model of reality is projecting the outside world to us.

Depending on the specific problem, there are often a number of gold nuggets in terms of resources which we can utilise to shape their model of reality. This often forms the basis for bypassing as much resistance as possible to belief change or concept reconstruction.

For a personal consultation visit: www.themindhealer.co.uk

Again you will see countless examples of this moving forward. It will make more sense seeing it in action than can be described theoretically.

The Teaching of New Skills

This most often comes in the form of communication advice and interpersonal skills. I remember working alongside an NHS Cognitive Behaviour Therapist with a boy suffering from quite severe social anxiety. I remember they had given the boy some advice to force himself to begin conversations with random people.

No indication was given about what to say however. The hidden assumption being that conversation was easy and that all he had to do was to overcome the fear and do it. My preference is to give very specific help and advice in this situation. I will tell them exactly what to say and how to say it. We will both come up with something that they feel comfortable with and they can begin with baby steps.

In many therapies and modalities there is a presupposition that we all have everything we need to achieve what we want to achieve. There may be an element of truth to this but, in my experience, starting people off with specifics is far quicker and more effective.

For a personal consultation visit: www.themindhealer.co.uk

Identification of Tasks to Be Carried Out

This often comes hand in hand with the previous task of teaching new skills. Once a new skill has been learned, the client has to go out into the world and carry out the new skill in the form of a task. Tasks can be a very powerful way to amend a model of reality and sometimes the right task at the right moment can be the piece of work which makes all of the difference for a client.

Depending on the nature of the problem, tasks aren't always relevant. Other times PSTEC or cognitive work is required prior to the carrying out of any tasks. The key is to know the full range of tools you have at your disposal and as a result, you will have the best chance of creating lasting change for yourself or others.

Summary

In this section I began by outlining how our experience of the world isn't how things actually are. We are the victims of our life experiences and many of our beliefs and ways of being stem from historical events over which we had little control.

I recommended viewing beliefs and our perception of the world as being just a vague approximation of what is actually out there. Therefore it makes sense to view our existing beliefs as something which might be replaced with better and more functional ways of thinking, as opposed to determine whether a belief is true or false. This then sets up the optimal frame of

For a personal consultation visit: www.themindhealer.co.uk

mind with which to make change with the least amount of resistance from our model of reality.

I then talked about how this way of viewing the mind creates the perfect background for any work on emotions, beliefs and concepts. Various methods and ideas were presented with the aim of getting a person's model of reality as open as possible for change before any direct work has been done. I briefly outlined how the lesser used methods of identifying resources, teaching new skills and setting tasks can be used in conjunction with everything that was explained beforehand to really ramp up the power of everything as a whole. I also hinted that sometimes these peripheral approaches can sometimes be the key to change.

Next I will begin digging much deeper into the model of reality. If some of what I wrote about concepts and beliefs left you scratching your head, I suspect that the numerous case studies that follow will elucidate these ideas, allowing you to see them in action in the real world with real people.

For a personal consultation visit: www.themindhealer.co.uk

Belief Change, Concept Restructure and Reframes

This is quite a large chapter and I have included a lot of information in here. Before we get to the problem specific case studies I thought it prudent to go into more detail on this particular topic. Getting a good grasp of these ideas now will make future chapters more understandable when you finally do see the process in full flow.

A client's awareness of the general ideas described so far has a big impact on their willingness and ability to change. They put the therapist and client in the very powerful position of both observing the "problem" as though it were something external to either of us and then we co-create solutions and test them out.

Reframes are an extremely powerful way of changing a person's perception of a problem. By analysing the current perception, different viewpoints can be identified and "tried on" to see how they fit and feel. I often have my client take part in this process as we come up with different ways of looking at the situation. Sometimes a simple direct reframe can be enough to obliterate a problem.

For a personal consultation visit: www.themindhealer.co.uk

Miss E - school refuser

One striking example of this is Miss E. She had been through a lot but the focus of one session was her school attendance. She was pretty much classed as a school refuser but on this particular day she happened to be in and was happy to see me. Through conversation it quickly became clear that the word "school" had quite strong negative emotions linked with it.

I tried to ascertain what it was about school that she didn't like so much but she just shrugged. I asked if it was the pupils, the teachers, the building itself or something else. She said that it isn't anything specific and she doesn't mind it when she is here but just the thought of "school" makes her angry and anxious.

My usual mode of operation at this point after the pre-talk would have been to identify when this began and clear emotions linked to this. However this wasn't my first session with her and we had already cleared a great deal of baggage by this point.

There was something about the way she said "school" that led me to believe that the concept itself was highly emotionally charged in and of itself. I jokingly asked if it just the word "school" that she disliked and she laughed, saying that it really is and when her mother is shouting for her to get ready for "school" it really winds her up.

I suggested that we emotionally de-charge the word school with a Click Track but she had a reluctance to do so. This would have involved just thinking about school in general or even just the word itself whilst running a Click Track. I sensed that the reluctance was more a lack of desire to do a Click Track at that point in time rather than a reluctance to let go of the bad feelings associated with school.

I asked what she wanted to do when she left school and she said that she wanted to work in a care home as she enjoys caring for and looking after people. I suggested that in a way school is a place where children are cared for and looked after. I had good rapport and knew she valued my help so I pointed out that it was school that had got me in to help her and some of the other children. She agreed that this actually was the case.

Within the framework you read about in the introduction, this is an example of identifying resources within a person's model of reality. Through questions and conversations it appeared that the concept of "care" was a strongly positive one within Miss E's model of reality and so I thought it might be useful to borrow and utilise it on the problematic inner representation she had of "school".

I asked her to imagine for a moment that school wasn't called "school". She actually enjoyed learning so I suggested that school is place where she can do something she enjoys and that it is full of people - teachers and pupils - who care about her and like her. I asked how she would feel if she came here but that it was a "care home" that she was coming to where she learned and spent time with her friends. She immediately said, "I want to call it care place" and a small grin spread across her face.

For a personal consultation visit: www.themindhealer.co.uk

I asked her how she would feel each morning having to get up and go to "care place". She said she could imagine her mother shouting her to get ready for "care place" and it just didn't bother her at all (before she was getting agitated at the mere thought of this).

I am aware that she definitely continued to go to school for the rest of that week but it was coming up to summer holidays and so at this point I have no idea as to the longevity of that piece of work. Ideally we would have emotionally de-charged the concept of "school" either with the emotional clearing Click Tracks or a PSTEC Negative on "I have the belief that school is a bad place" and maybe ran a PSTEC Positive about enjoying school. The exact wording of both would have to be discussed and agreed upon with Miss E if it had come to this.

The purpose of this case study is to illustrate how very real the idea that "The Map is not the Territory" is in a literal sense. It also gives an example of how we can identify a resource already within a person's model of reality and utilise it to neutralise a problem concept.

Miss L - homework anxiety

Miss L enjoyed school but the idea and thought of homework made her very anxious. I questioned her to see exactly how the problem manifested and she said that she literally felt completely fine up until the end of school. She would then suddenly feel very anxious which would remain until she completed her homework.

For a personal consultation visit: www.themindhealer.co.uk

She had already tried a Click Track when feeling the anxiety as her mother had downloaded it for her but this didn't seem to have any impact. At this point I may have identified when exactly this began to see if there were any specific triggers. I may have done some digging to see if there were any problematic beliefs keeping the anxiety trapped in place.

However I decided to first attempt some gentle restructuring of her model of reality around the topic of homework. I confirmed with her that she has zero anxiety all the way up to the end of her last lesson. By this point she was already aware of the nature of the mind and therefore was wide open to new ways of looking at the scenario. I suggested that she pretended that school finished later than it currently does but that the last lesson takes place at home and she has her mother there to help her. This resonated with Miss L immediately and the anxiety never came back when doing homework. This is another example of identifying something already existing within a model of reality which has neutral or good feelings towards it (in this case the lessons in school) and simply re-categorising the problem structure within it.

Mr G - diabetes anger and resentment

Mr G had diabetes and was very bitter and angry at this fact. He felt justified in these feelings and had a little resistance to letting go. However after a brief talk he agreed that this anger and bitterness weren't serving any useful purpose and therefore would be better gone. As anyone reading this will be aware, just because you decide a feeling isn't helping at all doesn't mean that

For a personal consultation visit: www.themindhealer.co.uk

your brain will just let go. In other words his conscious resistance had been bypassed but we needed to get past the guards and make some changes deeper within his castle/model of reality.

We ran a Click Track on the anger he felt when focusing on the fact that he has diabetes and it came right down after one listen. There was still some background resentment there though. I could have potentially ran another Click Track but decided to do some probing first. I asked what it was specifically about having diabetes that bothers him the most.

For him it was purely the time spent having to inject himself each day. I asked how long it actually took and he admitted that it only took a minute or two. By this point he was already aware of the model of reality and how it can massively influence how we experience everything. I suggested that he has to brush his teeth twice a day which probably took longer. He probably has dozens of other essential tasks that he has to carry out each day and I asked if he gets himself wound up about them. He didn't so I had him to imagine it was just an extension of brushing his teeth. This simple reframe removed his resentment. We were short on time and normally I would have reinforced this change with a PSTEC Positive statement such as "From now on I can feel calm injecting as it is just like brushing my teeth" or similar but he would have played an active role in identifying the specific words used. This was a schoolboy and therefore with the feedback opportunity that that allows for, I learned that a month on he still felt neutral towards the idea of having to inject.

For a personal consultation visit: www.themindhealer.co.uk

If I had gone in straight away with this reframe I don't think it would have made much of an impact. However my pre-talk put him in a frame of mind that would be much more open to ideas such as this. We identified resources within his model of reality that were similar but neutral emotionally and in a sense re-categorised the notion of injecting, thus releasing the resentment.

Mr A - I am not a real person

Mr A had been through a huge amount of trauma and had spent years in therapy without much improvement before seeing me. I shall miss out most of what occurred as I want to focus on a particularly relevant statement he made which pertains to this chapter.

He said, "I am not a real person" and that he therefore feels as though everything he does and says is an act. He was aware of the model of reality and nature of beliefs by this point and was open to discussing what, "I am not a real person" meant within his model of reality. He was unable to give an answer to what was meant by "real" and even "person". He felt that his head was full of wool and that if he let his mask slip people would see that there was nothing there behind the mask.

He agreed that this belief wasn't working for him and was up for analysing it and coming up with a better one. In an attempt to identify resources we set about asking what positive attributes his friends might say about him. At first he couldn't think of any so I started off with some things that I had noticed about him such as a great sense of humour and a warm personality. When stuck in

For a personal consultation visit: www.themindhealer.co.uk

the "reality tunnel" of "I am not a real person" all of these positive traits were completely invisible and out of his awareness.

He admitted that when taking these things into consideration, he possibly was a real person but still didn't feel like one and his head still felt full of wool. We created what I call a "belief bucket" and wrote down any belief and thought linked to the key disempowering thought. First we took a look at what currently existed in his model of reality that constituted being a real person and came up with something like this:

❖ Being similar to other people.
❖ Being more natural and automatic.
❖ Not analysing everything all of the time.
❖ Not working so much to rigid lists.
❖ Being able to switch off.

A background belief also cropped up about his partner which suggested that if she likes him, she too mustn't be a real person. But within the current reality tunnel this was countered by his thought that she likes him because of his mask and so she is actually a real person.

We both sat there looking at the list and he burst out laughing at how ridiculous it all sounded. However there was a very real issue to overcome as a part of him really did believe all of this. We came up with ideas of different ways of interpreting this "data" which would be more helpful and settled on one which was met with no resistance, at least consciously.

For a personal consultation visit: www.themindhealer.co.uk

He agreed that it would best if he thought of himself as a real person who is merely suffering from anxiety, possibly some of obsessive compulsive disorder traits and that he is just doing the best that he can.

The purpose of the belief bucket is to shine a torch on that particular part of the model of reality and see if any deeper/underlying beliefs become evident. This information can then be used moving forward. However even after uncovering all of this knowledge, it still seemed "I am not a real person" was a core belief that needed further work on.

He agreed to run a PSTEC Negative on this to weaken that belief structure. Prior to doing so we came up with a few potential replacement beliefs to implant straight after. This is something I often do as I believe it serves to increase desire and willingness to let go of the problem belief before the track is even run. He wrote down: "I have the belief that I am not a real person" and followed the instructions on PSTEC Negative. For any Cognitive Behaviour Therapists reading this, using PSTEC tools in this manner can really help bypass sticky problems such as these and seem to work very well when a person can see the falsehood of a belief but it still feels real to them.

Afterwards he said that the thought that he wasn't a real person just seemed laughable and that the feeling of "wool" in his head had gone. In later sessions we worked on his OCD and other issues but this work remained intact and he felt much more comfortable around other people and in himself as a result.

For a personal consultation visit: www.themindhealer.co.uk

Miss T - I feel as though I am trapped in a dark place

Miss T was a schoolgirl who had been raped and in a future chapter I shall describe exactly how I helped her. At this point I want to focus on something she said long after we had cleared much of the trauma. The court case was long gone, as was her anxiety and everything seemed to be going well for her in life. She had had a long period of happiness but requested to see me one day.

She said that she doesn't understand why, but she feels as though she is trapped in a dark place. Nothing specific had happened and I checked that all previous work we did remained intact and it was. She agreed that it doesn't seem to correspond with anything going on in her life. In her model of reality the words/concepts "trapped", "dark" and "place" seemed to be active, linked together and creating unpleasant feelings.

She agreed that it would best that we got her out of the dark place and on this occasion I decided to use PSTEC Negative on the presenting belief which was manifesting as a metaphor. She wrote down: "I have the belief that I am trapped in a dark place". Afterwards she felt calm and happy and said that the dark place is now gone.

I could have ran an emotion clearing Click Track on the image of her being trapped in a dark place. In fact in most cases there are multiple ways to solve the problem. Being completely aware of

For a personal consultation visit: www.themindhealer.co.uk

all the different approaches can give you confidence and increase the likelihood that success is attained.

Miss Z - vulnerability and weakness

There are various reasons why a person may struggle to hold down a relationship. I have helped many men and women who struggle in this area and for a small group of them, the cause is a tiny conceptual link in their model of reality. The cause will be slightly different in each case but ultimately the idea that expressions of kindness and vulnerability are linked with "weakness" in their mind. Weakness in these people often has a strong negative response associated with it.

Behind this is often a fear that if they are with a weak partner, others might see them as weak which is a dangerous thing in their mind. I won't go into the many different permutations and causes of this as I want to stay focused on how this can be restructured within their model of reality.

Once we have identified this pattern, the next question that arises is whether it is working for them in life or not. A consequence of viewing relationships through this reality tunnel is that an attraction to men who treat them unkindly is often a result; after all they may appear strong on the surface or, more importantly, at least not weak. Another consequence is that kind men who treat them well are inadvertently categorised as weak and therefore are pushed away.

For a personal consultation visit: www.themindhealer.co.uk

Once they are aware of this pattern of thought and behaviour we can begin to explore alternative ways of viewing what is going on that may produce more desirable results. I first begin to deconstruct their idea of what constitutes weakness. When you regularly come across a particular problem and have guided numerous people through this process, you can almost present to a client a ready-made alternative. It is important to keep them involved and be open to any suggestions they may have but this train of thought seems to work well in this scenario.

I suggest that if a man shows kindness and affection to them, in a sense he is in a position of vulnerability because they have the power to reject him. However just because they have the power to reject him, it doesn't make the client strong and the man weak in this scenario. In a sense, there is power in vulnerability. It takes strength to put yourself in that position without certainty of success. From this I suggest that a more accurate portrayal of what is occurring is the idea that vulnerability is a sign of strength.

For most people this makes complete sense and is at least as plausible as their original view point. We go through the pros and cons of adopting this as a new conceptual construct within their understanding of the world. Most realise that this will more likely result in a healthy long lasting relationship in which they are treated well and respected as well as feeling safe because they know they are with a strong person.

Some people really take these ideas on-board at an emotional level immediately and for these we create a PSTEC Positive statement to reinforce this new mode of thinking such as, "vulnerability really is a sign of strength" or "kindness is strength". The specific wording will be ultimately decided upon by the client and will be based on what feels right.

Other people might understand the new way of thinking intellectually but not feel it in their gut. For those I would likely begin with a PSTEC Negative on something such as: "I have the belief that vulnerability is a sign of weakness". After this they are much more likely to respond well to a PSTEC Positive statement affirming the new and better way of thinking.

Practical Advice on the use of PSTEC Positive and Negative

I feel now is a good time and place to touch upon some tips I have figured out along the way in using the belief change tracks optimally. As per the framework I described in the introduction, I would always begin with imparting knowledge about the nature of thought, beliefs and our mind. Next almost without fail I shall begin attacking any intense feelings using Click Tracks, even on topics which seem unrelated as a general rule of thumb. As I discuss in much more in-depth case studies in the following chapters, you will see how it all falls in place.

I actually prod the model of reality for information. It's a little like a vet pressing on different parts of an injured animal to find out where the pain is because of course the animal couldn't tell you itself.

For a personal consultation visit: www.themindhealer.co.uk

PSTEC Positive

With PSTEC Positive, once a statement is constructed it is to be read aloud 7 times after which they follow the instructions on the track. However I have them say it out loud 7 times as a test to see if it feels good, bad or neutral before even considering moving forward. As well as providing useful feedback, another benefit is that by saying it out loud, changes are already being made to the model of reality and I always ask if any other ideas or sentences come to mind, or maybe a rewording of the existing sentence once they have said it. It is also common that they get the idea to change maybe one word here or there, make it a bit shorter or longer. Once the change is made I have them say the new sentence out loud and repeat the process.

I have had some clients who have literally done this a dozen times before getting to the final PSTEC Positive track and you can almost guarantee that the final statement is perfect for them. They are normally buzzing before the track even starts. It's as if we are presenting the king of the castle with different paintings until he gets the perfect one and as a result feels great. Once the track is finished, we again look at it once more and assess whether it needs to be repeated or modified in any way. It is very common that slight modifications are made which ramp up the power of the track even more and further solidify the changes we are making to their model of reality.

There are some ultra-powerful general purpose statements that I have devised and tested which seem to really resonate with most people most of the time.

For a personal consultation visit: www.themindhealer.co.uk

"No matter what happens, everything is going to be ok"

This is an excellent one and is great way to end a session for people who have been through some major trials and tribulations who also have some uncertainty ahead. Prior to every PSTEC Positive use I always set the scene and pre-frame how the statement is to be understood. The pre-frame increases the chance that it will be taken on-board by their model of reality.

The pre-frame allows people to benefit from this statement in a scenario in which it is absolutely not clear that "everything is going to be ok". However I bypass any potential resistance caused by this by explaining that the fact of the matter is, life is full of ups and downs and this isn't meant to be denying that truth. I suggest interpreting it as adopting the attitude that whatever life throws at me, I will be able to handle it and in that sense, no matter what happens, everything (or I) will be ok.

I also suggest that when it comes to thinking about the future, although we have no idea what is going to happen, we can either imagine worst case scenarios and therefore torture ourselves with our own creations within our model of reality, or we can use the same faculty to produce feelings of calm and peace by visualising best case scenarios. Again this is often met with agreement from clients.

For some people in certain situations, this one statement is the only thinking that will budge them out of despair and emotional hell.

For a personal consultation visit: www.themindhealer.co.uk

Here are some more useful PSTEC Positive statements:

"I'll always be surrounded by people who love me"

One of our great communal fears seems to be uncertainty over the future which is addressed by the last statement. Another common one is the feeling of being alone or abandoned. This statement or its equivalent is great for making a person realise that they do have a network around them of people who care about them.

"I've got this"

This is a great one for people who have a goal to accomplish and it gives a sense of being in control of your own destiny. I got the idea from a boy who had suffered years of neglect and abuse, yet somehow, despite his suffering, he was a high achiever and very articulate. We were trying to come up with ideas of beliefs, statements or mottos which we could run a PSTEC Positive on. After some head scratching his eyes lit up and he lifted up his necklace and inscribed on it where the words, "I've got this".

He said it out loud seven times and this was clearly the right thought for him as just the act of saying it completely changed his physiology. He said it with a little aggression and determination on his face and we ran the thought through PSTEC Positive and he looked very different - his face was flushed and he was buzzing. He told me he was going to run to the head teacher and tell them the school must employ me as this

For a personal consultation visit: www.themindhealer.co.uk

is the first time in years of therapy that anything had worked. At the time I was on a trial day so I was quite happy with the result.

Since then I have suggested this as a possibility to many people, from those attempting to qualify for the Olympics, straight through to those about to do an exam or interview. Others, who are in a very unsettled place due to external circumstances, sometimes prefer it to "no matter what happens, everything is going to be ok". It is so critically important to listen to the information/feedback their models of reality give when coming up with potential ideas for statements as we are all unique.

In schools many of the children won't have access to PSTEC Positive to do any homework. As a good alternative I have them write the statement down three times a day, especially first thing in the morning and just before bed. Although not as good as using PSTEC Positive, it is a useful task to carry out in the weeks after a PSTEC Positive track has been used to increase the likelihood that it sticks.

In coming up with statements I'll often ask if they can think of a motto or mantra they can live by, especially if it is their external circumstances which are volatile. This last statement of "I've got this" is a great example of this and what separates this kind of statement from others is that it tends to have a higher positive emotional charge. You will see other examples of this in the chapters ahead.

For a personal consultation visit: www.themindhealer.co.uk

PSTEC Negative

As with PSTEC Positive I prod the model of reality to indirectly give me an idea of what is stored in there. In saying out loud a potential positive statement, if any subconscious resistance presents itself in the form of an unpleasant emotion, or even an inability to say out loud the agreed upon statement, this is a clear indication that one of two things are happening.

It could be that there is a strongly held belief already stored within the model of reality that completely counters the new belief that is being offered and is therefore blocking acceptance of it. Secondly it could be that there is a belief within the model of reality that adding in the new belief isn't safe.

Imagine someone is suffering from severe anxiety due to numerous traumas throughout their life. We would begin systematically removing the emotional baggage with the emotion Click Tracks, probably starting off with events which occurred earliest in life. The reason I would often do this is because their model of reality is less likely to oppose removal of them given the duration of time that has passed. Next imagine that they feel that the statement, "from now on I can feel calm and safe" would be a good one to run through PSTEC Positive. However when they come to say it out loud they aren't able to as something seems to be stopping them.

Next I would take a guess as to what belief is causing this. I have found that in many cases there is either a belief that it isn't safe

For a personal consultation visit: www.themindhealer.co.uk

to let go of the feeling, or that it is dangerous to feel safe. To check this I have them say out loud the opposite of this: "it is safe to let go of anxiety" or "it is safe to feel safe".

If this actually was the cause, subconscious resistance would flare up again and will have handed us on a plate the problematic reality tunnel to be disposed of with PSTEC Negative. However before doing so, I pre-frame the process so that there is as little conscious resistance as possible to letting go. I do this by explaining the nature of anxiety, how it is meant to protect us, that we do need it but sometimes it fires off more than is needed. I love the smoke alarm analogy that is often used to describe this. In the analogy our anxiety is likened to a smoke alarm in that it is essential and alerts us to danger to keep us safe.

However occasionally a fault develops which means that it fires off sometimes even when there is no danger present. I explain that the only consequence of letting go of the problem belief is that not only will they feel calmer and happier most of the time, but if anything does happen which requires their attention, they will likely be far better able to deal with it from a place of calm than they would in a state of panic.

Again I am hedging everything in the favour of change occurring and lasting. Once we have identified the problematic hidden belief we run it through PSTEC Negative. After experiencing PSTEC Negative, some people feel very different and notice immediate change. However a more typical response is that they feel confused.

For a personal consultation visit: www.themindhealer.co.uk

I remember the first time I used PSTEC Negative with a client, a teenage girl who had the belief that she was "vile and disgusting". This just so happened to be the words fired at her by bullies at primary school. Like many other people, after running this belief through PSTEC Negative she felt confused and nothing more. However when I saw her two weeks later, she had actually forgotten that we had done any work on this aspect of her anxiety and self-hate. It was only my questioning which made her realise and become aware that a week after I saw her, she had gone to a party and worn clothes she never would have had the confidence to wear. Only then did she realise that she felt far happier in herself and was at peace with how she looked. Huge change can actually occur without a person being aware of it, as it did in this case. This is why I always ask specifically what would be different in their lives if the problem disappeared.

So how do we know if PSTEC Negative has worked? One key method I use is to prod the model of reality once more and have them say out loud the statement they couldn't say, or experienced resistance to previously. Very often after PSTEC Negative it is either neutral or feels good. At this point we run through the process I described earlier in the PSTEC Positive section, in creating and testing new beliefs and ramping up the thoughts and modifying as and when needed.

I first talked about the value of saying out loud certain sentences or words in my book "PSTEC in the Trenches". However in that piece of work, it was used primarily to bring up emotion that was clearly there in a client but they were unable to bring it up on demand in order to run it through a Click Track. I feel that this new application of it is extremely important and shouldn't be

For a personal consultation visit: www.themindhealer.co.uk

overlooked. It can provide information about either your own or a client's model of reality which would be difficult to obtain in any other way.

How do these ideas sit alongside Cognitive Behaviour Therapy techniques? In a sense it is a mere extension of it. If for example it became clear that a client had a hidden belief that it wasn't safe to let go of anxiety, then we would identify and challenge the belief. However, especially with deep rooted and survival beliefs such as these I have found that challenging the belief alone isn't enough. The beauty of this approach is that we can challenge the belief and test if it has made a difference at the deeper level by having they say out loud the phrase again to see if the subconscious mind still produces a response. If it doesn't we can proceed and know that the work has stuck; if the subconscious mind still resists, we have an additional step to make the change at a deeper level.

Suicidal Clients

As you go through this piece of work you will hear how I have helped many suicidal people. However in this section I would just like to highlight something to look out for when someone says they are suicidal. Being "suicidal" is a complex abstract concept in the model of reality; in other words it is a higher level concept than something like table or chair which simply denotes an object. The higher you go up in levels of abstraction, the greater the chance that different people will utilise a word or language in general to denote something for which other people might infer something else.

One particular client I was working with would have bouts in which he would tell his loved ones that he was feeling "very suicidal". Of course this rings big alarm bells for anyone who may hear it and his family would often phone emergency suicidal help lines after which a crisis team would visit to help. However he always resented this help and the kind of things that were said to him during these times.

I decided to dig deeper and found out exactly what he meant by being "very suicidal" and so I asked that when he said it, was he was actually planning to take action. He looked at me shocked and said that he would never do that, he just meant that he was in a very low place.

I told him that when he told loved ones that he was "very suicidal", they genuinely thought there was a risk he was in danger. He was gobsmacked that this might be the case and I advised that in future he use words to describe how he is feeling which might not be confused with something more serious.

On another occasion I was asked to see a teenage boy in a school. However, I had to see him on the ground floor (normally the office I worked out of was on the first floor in that particular school) because by all accounts he was threatening to jump out of the window. As you can imagine there were some very worried staff and his parents were out of their minds.

Being very aware that the map is not the territory, I thought it prudent to question him to find out if we were all interpreting his words correctly. Like the client I described previously, he was shocked that people thought that he would actually do such a thing and explained that it was just his way of describing how low he felt.

Never assume that when a person says this that they don't mean it. However as you can see here, it might be an idea to dig a little deeper to see if there is any intention there or if it is just an expression of deep emotional pain. Either way, urgent help is needed.

For a personal consultation visit: www.themindhealer.co.uk

Grief

Being human is quite strange. The simple truth is that none of us really knows what happens after death. Losing a loved one is one of the most painful things we can go through and there is certainly a grieving process to go through. I vividly remember being preoccupied with the idea of death as a 12 year old, trying to grasp the enormity of the fact that it is something that we and all our loved ones will have to go through.

It isn't something I think much about these days. I am simply thankful for each and every day that I get with my family and friends. Obviously the facts of reality haven't changed so why do I feel and think differently about it now? Changes must have occurred in my model of reality, meaning that I experience specific concepts such as death in a more peaceful way.

Despite the intense pain we all feel when we lose a loved one, we all go through our own unique journey. For some, the grief will pass more quickly than for others and will be less intense and easier to deal with. Without help, others may still feel intensely upset decades on.

For a personal consultation visit: www.themindhealer.co.uk

In this chapter I will cover my latest thinking on helping those who are grieving as well as the very common fear of death. I decided to talk about the topic of grief early on because in it you will see many parts of the framework already described in action, which will help cement the knowledge you have already picked up. Grief often involves quite intense emotions and as such you will notice that PSTEC plays a key role in many of the case studies.

Unresolved Grief

Choosing whether to decrease the emotional pain of unresolved grief is a very personal one but there are three principles that I first wrote about in PSTEC in the Trenches that are worth quickly repeating.

First it is good to question the unwritten assumption that the amount of pain felt equals the amount of love felt for a person. The hidden logic goes that if the upset is removed, then in a sense, it is almost as if you loved the person less. I argue that a more useful way of looking at this is that with the upset reduced, it creates the space for more love. What was once too painful to think about now becomes something to revisit in your mind, reliving cherished memories, which often doesn't happen when the pain is too great. I liken this to reconnecting with the loved one.

Next I invite a person to think whether the person who has died would want them to suffer after the initial shock and, if so, for

For a personal consultation visit: www.themindhealer.co.uk

how long? Of course our loved ones would want us to suffer as little as possible whilst not forgetting them.

Finally I ask that if they themselves died, after the initial shock and upset that everyone would experience, how long would they want their loved ones to suffer for? I don't think many of us would want people to suffer, especially not loved ones. This trio of thought experiments is often enough for most people to agree that letting go of some of the pain might actually be a good idea.

Since "PSTEC in the Trenches" I have dealt with many dozens of people suffering from unresolved grief in all kinds of scenarios. Some of the grief is very recent, some long ago whilst for other people there is a loved one who is terminally ill. Others may have lost their loved one to suicide and this presents its own set of challenges for those left behind. Each person is unique and each situation warrants a slightly different approach.

The more recent the death, the more likely that PSTEC Positive statements will play a key role I have found.

Clients with a Terminally Ill Loved One

I have worked with numerous people who have a close family member who is likely to die in the very near future. Often, but not always, these people have a constant background feeling of upset/anxiety/grief.

For a personal consultation visit: www.themindhealer.co.uk

With these clients I explain that our work together is a little more experimental than would be the case, for example, if we were working on unresolved grief on someone who has already passed away a long time ago. For those people, the results and methodology are more predictable and straightforward.

The reason I frame this as experimental is that during the initial Click Tracks, some people can become more upset than they actually were at the start of the track. Without this pre-frame they may come to the incorrect conclusion that this work isn't helping when, in reality, an increase in upset is valuable information for moving forward.

If the person is completely overwhelmed to begin with, I explain that the purpose of the track is not to make them indifferent to the current situation but rather, to take some of the steam out of their system so they feel calmer, despite everything. In fact this is a key perspective I like to instil when helping anyone in this kind of scenario, as making the process about "releasing steam" reduces the risk of any resistance cropping up compared with framing it in another way.

If their background overwhelm is constantly very high, I have the person think about something other than their loved one. For example I have them think about day to day stresses or even something historical and focus the Click Track on that. This is to give their minds something to focus on and by clearing some bad feelings from their system, it can help them indirectly feel a little better. I have found that if they don't focus on anything in

For a personal consultation visit: www.themindhealer.co.uk

particular, the words on the track often draw their minds to the current situation which can overwhelm them further.

A more recent technique I have come up with for allowing Click Tracks to do their work on scenarios which are too highly charged to focus on directly, is to have them imagine writing a few words on a piece of paper which represents, at an abstract level, the object of upset. For example a person could imagine writing "upset about current situation", then imagine folding it up and focus on this imaginary folded piece of paper throughout the track.

I have found that this allows the track to do its work without bringing up as much overwhelm. Afterwards they may feel calm thinking about the situation directly or, if not, it will likely be much lower than it would have been to start with and possibly allow work to be done directly on it. In a sense it is like pointing the track at a less sensitive part within their model of reality. I will talk more about this in the section on trauma.

A free basic Click Track or an EEF Click Track can be used for this. It is also possible to use Click Track 2015 but I would fast forward much of the audio so it gets right to the tapping instructions, so that they just focus on the one specific thing rather than multiple instances of the same emotion.

I would apply these tracks a few times to get the feelings as low as possible. I believe a few more case studies will best clarify how I proceed from here, depending on the outcome of the initial

For a personal consultation visit: www.themindhealer.co.uk

emotion clearing tracks and how I incorporate PSTEC Positive and when to use it.

As in every case we are all unique but there are certain things to consider in these scenarios. Certain approaches tend to be more effective than others depending on time scales involved.

A prognosis of 12 or more months into the future:

Mr G

Mr G had a grandfather who was diagnosed with a terminal illness with the doctor giving a figure of around 12 months left to live. Mr G was very close to his grandfather and was distraught at the thought of what was to come. In fact he couldn't even think of the situation without becoming very emotional.

With no intervention, Gary's last 12 months with his grandfather would have been greatly hampered by his negative feelings. In fact he may have even seen him less than he would have done otherwise, because he found the prognosis so difficult to accept.

This was a straightforward case. I explained that the aim of the track is merely to take some of the steam out of his system and we went ahead with a Click Track. It took just one and he felt calm. Gary emailed me 18 months later saying that he had felt remarkably calm after the session, which lasted. His grandfather had just died and although he was upset, it was much more manageable than it would have been without using the Click Track. However he wanted to speak at the funeral but was worried in case he would be too upset to speak.

For a personal consultation visit: www.themindhealer.co.uk

To overcome this he used PSTEC Positive on the following statement, "I will feel calm and confident when speaking at the funeral". He used this a few times a day in the lead up to the funeral and on the day he felt the usual emotions people often feel at funerals, but a sense of calm came over him the moment he got up to talk about his grandfather and he did a great job. He emailed a few weeks later to say that he is still sad but in a way feels at peace with what has happened.

Even with feelings of calm, I do not necessarily consider the grieving to be over but whatever your unique journey through the grieving process is, from my perspective it is better to feel calmer.

To sum up, as one would expect, the longer a person has left to live, the more likely the standard Click Tracks and EEF's will make a big impact on their own.

A prognosis of months or less left to live:

As we approach the final stretch of time, the emotion clearing Click Tracks tend to be a bit more hit and miss and more of a need for PSTEC Positive will arise. Because things get a little trickier in these scenarios, I shall give more case studies to show my thinking and how I approach these more complex situations.

Miss P - terminally ill auntie

Miss P was very close to her auntie who apparently had two months left to live. She was devastated and very overwhelmed, constantly on the verge of tears in my office. Because her overwhelm was so high I decided to hunt for other traumas to see if there was anything else that was emotionally charged to start with. I think the analogy of the emotional barrel sums up this perfectly; as we go through life, if anything negative occurs which we aren't quite able to deal with, our emotional barrel gets filled a little. Over time this can become more and more full and once it gets near to the top we are very overwhelmed, often constantly teary, may experience panic attacks and our sleep may be disrupted.

By applying the Click Tracks to any event which is emotionally charged and therefore contributing to the pain felt, a reduction of pain is often noticed towards everything else also. In identifying possible contributors to their emotional barrel, I nearly always ask if they had experienced any of the following:

Lost any other loved ones
Victim of bullying
Victim of any other emotional or physical violence
Any health scares of self or loved ones
Any one off traumas like a car accident
Any big fall outs with important people in their life
Any big family changes like parental separation
Any other event in their life which was or is still painful emotionally

I also tend to ask if they hate themselves. Many people do and clearing this is a key starting point to reduce any potential sabotage from a part of them that thinks that they don't deserve to be happy.

For a personal consultation visit: www.themindhealer.co.uk

In Miss P's case, she had a very poor relationship with her mother and felt intense anger towards her. She had also been bullied 5 years previously but this was nothing compared to the anger felt towards her mother. Nothing specific or major had happened with her mother, it seemed more a case of small niggles building up over time into something huge.

There was a little reluctance initially but she agreed that letting go of this anger would be a good thing. It started off as 10/10 anger which completely disappeared after two Click Tracks. This substantially reduced the upset and overwhelm she felt overall.

Next we ran the medium length Click Track 2015 on the 5/10 upset she still felt about her auntie as well as historical bullying. All of this disappeared and she couldn't believe how calm she felt about the situation. It is impossible to say for sure, but I suspect if we had gone straight for the presenting issue at the start, we may have been met with far more resistance. By clearing other big emotional thorns first, it gave her the breathing space to process and deal with everything. With the emotion towards mother gone I then went on and gave her specific advice on repairing the relationship with her which she was keen to try out.

This session is quite recent and at present I am unaware how she is doing. We had run out of time, otherwise I would have liked to end with a PSTEC Positive track or two. In this next case study you will see how I applied PSTEC Positive to create a very powerful intervention.

For a personal consultation visit: www.themindhealer.co.uk

Miss C

Miss C was a 15 year old girl in a state of constant high anxiety and panic attacks. Her father had been told that he had a matter of months left and he was deteriorating noticeably by the day. To make matters worse, her mother had agoraphobia and had barely left the house for 20 years. There were no other major traumas in her life. In this instance I made Miss C aware that the aim of the first Click Track was to take some of the steam out of her system. As always in these situations, I also framed the entire process as a series of experiments, just in case it temporarily lead to greater upset.

In this instance she began with a 10/10 anxiety. Rather than focus directly on her father, I had her focus on school stress which was high. It took three Click Tracks after which she felt very calm, despite everything.

We ran out of time but I was told that the following 3 weeks she was feeling calm overall. However on the 4th week her father took a turn for the worse and she came into my office with an anxiety of about 6/10 which was still far less than it was when she first came to see me. Her father had since overcome this dip but it was still a bit of a shock so we ran a Click Track and, once more, she became calm. However, this time we had time to construct a PSTEC Positive statement to increase the chances of our work lasting longer as well as reduce any turbulence that may crop up as things progress.

For a personal consultation visit: www.themindhealer.co.uk

We used one of the "power statements" I described earlier in the book. This was:

"No matter what happens, everything is going to be ok".

We tested variations of this but she felt this wording was the best for her at this point in time. I gave a brief pre-frame to ensure she realised that his wasn't an attempt to kid herself but rather to instil the attitude that whatever life does throw at her, she will be able to deal with it. This gave her a sense of empowerment and resilience and we repeated the same sentence several times. She said that she felt a deeper calmness than when we used the Click Tracks alone.

Following this, we identified a viewpoint which had an even deeper calming influence on her. This was: "Perhaps my father will live far longer than any of us imagine". This was prefaced with the fact that we can use our imagination to bring us peace or pain and that running this through PSTEC Positive could do only good (once we had determined that her model of reality agreed that this was a useful thought by having her say it out loud to see what response it gave).

I had a "check in" with her two months later and despite a few more ups and downs with her father, she had dealt with it very well. She left school shortly after and so I wasn't able to see how she and her father were doing but I suspect the work we did together would have made the difficult time she was facing a little easier to deal with.

For a personal consultation visit: www.themindhealer.co.uk

Miss Y

When I first met Miss Y she was extremely stressed as she was about to do her GCSE's. However 6 months previously she had broken her ankle and due to complications, she was in and out of hospital every week, missing lots of vital classwork. She was having regular panic attacks and barely sleeping. In our pre-talk it was clear that something major was going on in her life other than this but she found it too distressing to even voice at this point. To take her out of overwhelm we ran a few Click Tracks whilst focusing on the stress of school and her current situation. This brought her out of overwhelm but any mention of the other "topic", even to work on content free, was still a little too raw so we left it there at that point.

In the next session she plucked up the courage to tell me that her mother had been diagnosed with a terminal illness 5 years ago and was told at the time that she had around 5 years left to live. Sadly this prophecy was proving accurate. In addition to the trouble she was having with her ankle, she had two very young sisters, she had never met her father and the only other relative nearby was her grandfather who thankfully she had a good relationship with.

All in all it was a very sad and stressful situation for anyone to be in, let alone a teenage girl. We used the Click Tracks a few times which did bring the anxiety/upset down from a 10/10 to around a 6/10. However it soon came back as soon as she thought of the situation. So far, within the framework, we had gone through the pre-talk about the nature of thoughts and beliefs. We had

For a personal consultation visit: www.themindhealer.co.uk

attempted to run the emotion tracks on both lesser traumas as well as the main cause of the upset.

The next stage was to figure out a new way of thinking about the situation which feels more peaceful by comparison with the existing viewpoint. We had a long chat and it was clear that, in essence, she feared losing the feeling of being loved from her life. Next we set about seeking out resources already within her model of reality, which could be utilised to ease this pain. Through conversation, it became clear that she was very close to her sisters and grandfather and felt loved by them. She also had a very strong friendship group. With this knowledge we considered different options, tested them out by saying them out loud and rewording it until it felt perfect. The one we finally decided on was:

"I will always be surrounded by people who love me"

Prior to this, we had already tried "no matter what happens everything will be ok" and although it did feel positive, we decided to test some more out first. Even just saying the new statement out loud seven times she felt a definite change. After running it through PSTEC Positive, all her anxiety had gone. We had some more time so she ran through it a few more times and by the end of the session she felt at peace.

Like the girl in the previous case study, I saw her a few months on and to my amazement we had to do zero work on her mother. Rather she was feeling anxious about her exams!

For a personal consultation visit: www.themindhealer.co.uk

Mr J

This is a great example of when you really need to dig deep within a person's model of reality to identify resources which can be utilised. Whilst there are certain statements which seem to resonate with most people, sometimes we have to create a statement which would probably only ever work for that person's unique model of reality and this is one of those times.

Mr J had major anger. Like many who possess more anger in their system than they would like, he had been bullied historically. We worked through this and other causes of anger and it made a huge impact in specific contexts. However, there was still a lot of background anger which I discovered was due to his Nan being terminally ill. Upset and unresolved grief is an extremely common cause of anger and it seems that many find anger a little easier to deal with and so it often seems to sit on top of the upset.

He was very close to his Nan and she was expected to have a month or maybe two left at the most. In telling me this, a huge wave of grief swept over him and he was very distressed. Mr J had previously achieved a lot of success with the Click Tracks and loved doing them and how they made him feel calm. I explained that with all of this being so current and on-going that we need to view it more as an experiment to see what happens. I have experimented greatly with having client's assume success or hint that more work might need to be done and I have found that the latter is by far the best approach.

He started off with 10/10 upset. Because we had worked on other things already and there was no other historical baggage or stress to deal with, we decided to go straight for the topic at hand. The first Click Track brought the upset down a little half way through the track only for it to come up again at the end. We ran it again but this time rather than think of his current situation, he imagined writing down "situation with Nan" and focused on that idea rather than on reality directly. Half way through he wanted to stop and came to the conclusion that it wouldn't work on this issue.

Because I framed the entire thing as a series of experiments he had hadn't given up at this point and we set to work on possible PSTEC Positive statements. His Nan was in a lot of pain so I suggested maybe a statement which focused on the fact that she will soon be at peace/out of pain. I gave possibilities around the idea of him dealing with it better than he imagined, along the lines of "no matter what happens everything will be ok". None of these ideas, nor others we came up, with resonated with him.

In the search for useful concepts/ideas/words/resources that may provide some comfort within his model of reality, I asked him what his favourite memories were of his Nan. He listed off several and one in particular seemed to have a big calming impact on him as his face lit up and he was smiling at the memory. I learned that this was a holiday in which the whole family had had a great time. I also learned that this was the last holiday his Nan had with her own daughter, who died shortly after.

For a personal consultation visit: www.themindhealer.co.uk

The key ideas and concepts which sprung out from this conversation was that he believed in heaven, that his Nan would soon be with her daughter and also the idea of freedom and laughter were particularly positively charged in this context. We constructed a statement involving these ideas and I had him say them out loud seven times to see how it felt. It felt quite calming but he had an idea of a word to change in the sentence and we repeated the process. Once again, a slight revision of the sentence occurred and when he said that out loud, it felt good to him. The final sentence was something along the lines of:

"Soon Nan will be laughing again with (daughter's name) just like we were on holiday"

We ran this through PSTEC Positive and at the end he had a huge grin on his face. All his pain had disappeared to his amazement. We repeated PSTEC Positive on the same sentence a few times with the intention of locking it in place more fully. Despite the obvious success he said that he didn't expect it to last. I advised keeping a sense of curiosity about how things will go as otherwise his expectation could actually cause the distress to come back.

I saw him a month later and I had never seen him so relaxed. He said he just feels grateful for every extra day that he gets with his Nan now and has no sorrow. In other words his model of reality appeared to have completely accepted the inevitable and so he felt a sense of peace. He said he knew he was going to be ok after our session because two days later, a boy was trying to wind him up about his Nan. In the past this would have resulted in a

For a personal consultation visit: www.themindhealer.co.uk

definite fight but instead he ignored it and got on with his day without any upset.

The Immediate Aftermath of Grief

As I mentioned earlier, grieving as well as the philosophical/religious views that go along with it are very personal so it is entirely up to the individual if they want to experience a little release from what can be an overwhelming and suffocating mental pain. As with those who are terminally ill, distance in time from the actual event plays a big role in how to deal with it using tools such as PSTEC as well as other methods. I always explain my perception of grief and then it is up to the client if he/she wants to attempt to alleviate the suffering.

A few years ago I had direct experience of this. After the bereavement I was able to go into work and on the surface I am pretty sure no-one would have had a clue that inside, my stomach was churning constantly, I had a constant lump in my throat and felt a suffocating heaviness. Personally I'm not really into suffering when there is help at hand so it took around 4 Click Tracks to bring my 10/10 overwhelm down to a 0/0. I felt calm. By no means did this mean I was completely ok or that I was over the grieving process. However, it did mean that my day to day life became much calmer and that I could process the situation at a more leisurely pace. If I had really wanted to I could have spent time digging deep within my model of reality to figure out resources or viewpoints I could utilise. However, because the

For a personal consultation visit: www.themindhealer.co.uk

Click Tracks were bringing it down slowly but surely, I decided to continue down that route and was happy with it as it was.

Miss K

Miss K had lost her husband two months ago. Her suffering was very intense and she felt like she needed some breathing space. I discovered that there was a particular image of her husband in her head just before his death that haunted her. Rather than focus on the entirety of the situation I had her focus on that one thing. Two Click Tracks later, the image had lost all of its emotional charge. This had a huge knock on effect and made her feel much calmer overall. Despite some pain still being there, it was at a level that she could cope with and actually wanted to keep hold of it at that point so we did no further work.

Mr P

Mr P was a 16 year old whose father had committed suicide 2 months previously. His life had been happy and carefree when, 6 months ago, his father began taking drugs. Literally, from day one, his father became another person. He was physically and emotionally abusive and often stole money from his own children to fund his habit. Four months on he was found hung in his room.

Two weeks ago Mr P had split up from his partner of over a year (which is quite a long relationship at that age), had been the victim of cyber-bullying and was self-harming. Moreover, his stepfather was being very emotionally abusive towards him when his mother wasn't around. In other words Mr P was in a very bad place and really struggling to stay afloat.

Fortunately most people who lose a loved one don't have all of this additional drama to deal with. However, my approach with Mr P is one I often use with people who have recently lost a loved one. We began working on emotionally charged events that are completely unrelated to the death of the loved one. Using the Click Tracks we cleared the anger and upset surrounding historical bullying as well as the more recent cyber-bullying. Next we worked on removing anger and upset over the actions of his stepfather. This work had brought him down from a constant 10/10 about everything to a general background anxiety and upset of about 6/10 and he was able to breathe properly without the heaviness there for the first time in many months.

Next, rather than deal with the upset and grief about his father, we focused on the anger he felt towards his father for his behaviour in those final months. As I always do when it comes to anger, I explain that in removing anger it isn't about forgiveness and that he can think what he wants about his father whether the anger is present or not. I liken it to getting rid of a headache, only rather than a headache it is the physical sensations of anger. He was able to bring up an 8/10 of anger. One medium length Click Track 2015 cleared not only anger but any shred of upset. He felt calm for the first time in a long time and couldn't quite believe it. He was also unable to bring up any bad feeling about anything even when trying to. We had ran out of time and so weren't able to seek out useful PSTEC Positive statements to end the session with.

For a personal consultation visit: www.themindhealer.co.uk

I suspect a little more work will be required with Mr P moving forward but this case study offers a repeat of the valuable lesson already shown. If anything is too traumatic or overwhelming to deal with, identify other emotionally charged events/situations/memories in their lives and work on them. If you clear everything but the main trauma, if the trauma hasn't already been cleared indirectly, it is often much easier to target directly.

Unresolved Grief from a Long Time Ago

Many of the same principles described above can be applied here. The main difference being that it is often much easier to clear with the standard Click Tracks. However there are definitely occasions in which either a person hasn't yet been able to grieve for the loved one and so the feelings are very intense, or that, despite grieving, the intensity of upset remains very high even decades later.

Miss J

Miss J had been through some severe hardships in her life. One of the more relatively minor issues in her life was unresolved grief over a grandparent who died 20 years ago. In most cases any upset like this from so long ago would be removed after one or two listens of a Click Track. However I am highlighting this case because there was a little more to it. Unexpectedly, anger came right up so we worked on that first, when it became clear that it was the top of an emotional pyramid (a situation in which

For a personal consultation visit: www.themindhealer.co.uk

one or more emotions are sitting on top of each other), with a mass of upset underneath. Two more EEF Click Tracks had no impact on the upset which is unusual for something so long ago.

In the search to discover what concepts/ideas/beliefs were propping up this upset we discussed the circumstances around it. Miss J had blamed herself over a situation that had occurred which resulted in her grandfather having to move out of the house and live alone. I detected that the idea of loneliness was highly charged in Miss J's model of reality and either needed amending as a concept in itself or we needed to construct a new meaning about that period of time which removed the idea of loneliness.

Firstly I attempted to identify viewpoints which may question the initial perception of her grandfather being lonely. Miss J had never thought about this but, through conversation, realised that actually her grandfather probably saw her family just as much as before but just slept in a different house. Also that sleeping in a different house had benefits in that he had his own space and probably had more freedom; another concept which appeared important to Miss J. My intention was to have us devise a PSTEC Positive statement which reframed the memory of her grandfather in terms of freedom whilst maintaining a strong bond with her family (in other words leaving the concept of "loneliness" out of the equation).

However, the conversation itself was enough to restructure this particular part of her model of reality in a way which led her to feelings of peace rather than distress. As can be seen time and

For a personal consultation visit: www.themindhealer.co.uk

again, each of our models of reality are unique and there is no one rule that fits all. The intensity of the upset in this case would have led me to initially believe that further work might be required. Despite this, perhaps through a combination of the pre-talk reducing resistance along with taking on different perspectives for size, and the reshaping of the meanings involved within the trauma, the changes occurred through conversation alone and lasted.

Mr L - Highly Hypnotisable Client

Earlier in the book I talked about the idea of some people having a model of reality which is very easy to amend and that we can refer to these people as highly hypnotisable. Here is one such example in the realm of unresolved grief. Mr L came into my office and I was told beforehand that he had recently lost a great grandparent. Of course bouts of intense emotion can hit someone suffering from unresolved grief for a long time after but the intensity of emotion he was demonstrating lead me to suspect that the death had happened very recently.

His great grandmother had died 6 months ago and to my surprise he said he had never been close to her and hadn't seen her much. At the moment he said this he took a photograph of her out of his wallet and became very upset. The intensity of upset for someone he didn't really know, with the absence of other aggravating factors led me to suspect that this might not be a typical scenario.

He agreed it might be worth trying a Click Track but within 30 seconds he became too upset to continue. He had also just told me that he had been studying the different stages of grief, trying to figure out what level he was at.

I concluded that he may be a highly hypnotisable client and went completely off topic and asked him what his favourite holiday or experience had been in life. He looked at me strangely but began to answer anyway. Within 30 seconds he was animatedly describing some of his favourite memories with a glint in his eyes and a grin from ear to ear.

I next asked what he planned on doing over the Easter holidays and he excitedly told me some of his plans, after which he opened his wallet, took out the photograph and began crying once more.

I explained that some people are very responsive to their own thoughts. I asked if he thought his great gran would want him to suffer to which he replied no. He agreed that by carrying around the photograph and frequently looking at it, knowing what response it would generate, is very similar to someone repeatedly touching a hot flame; i.e. no useful purpose with lots of pain as a result.

He began asking me more questions about the stages of grief. I advised him to forget about the stages of grief for now and to focus on things he is looking forward to. I also advised him to write down a list of things he was looking forward to everyday for the next few weeks. I gave him the behavioural task of reading out this list if he found himself gravitating towards the dark thoughts. A month later I saw him and he was completely fine.

What led me to suspect a highly hypnotisable client in this case was the intensity of upset for someone he didn't know that well and hadn't been close to. I tested my hypothesis by asking him questions which would force his mind to seek out positive experiences/emotions within his model of reality. The dramatic change which resulted from these questions confirmed to me that treating him as a highly hypnotisable client might obtain the best results. If he answered the positive and happy questions whilst maintaining feelings of upset, I would have continued to go through the procedures I have talked about previously in this chapter.

Working Directly With a Terminally Ill Person

Each time I have worked with a terminally ill person, my approach has been the same. I initially ignore the fact that they are terminally ill and begin a cleansing of their "emotional barrel", clearing away as much historic and current unresolved conflict as possible. This on its own often produces a huge change in their state.

At present I have only worked with a handful of people in this predicament and so don't have a huge list of case studies to draw from to illustrate points. However once historical emotional trauma has been removed, the next step will depend on the person's model of reality, how the concept of death is structured in their mind and any views they have as to what, if anything, comes next.

The people I have worked with have felt quite at peace overall and accepting of their fate, despite a few wobbles here or there. Some have come to terms with their death but have a fear of sickness and pain. In these cases it is a matter of Click Tracking any negative feelings attached to those thoughts as well as coming up with PSTEC Positive statements which resonate with them about being able to cope no matter what.

Others may be more concerned with how their loved ones will cope once they have gone. Again we would identify the key problematic concepts within their model of reality, look for resources, potential re-categorisations and alternative viewpoints. Next we would test some of them out until we came up with the one that produced the most acceptance. Also PSTEC Positive statements which create the attitude that they can deal with anything that is thrown at them like "no matter what happens, everything is going to be ok" would be useful. The beauty of this statement, in particular, is that it is quite vague and can be interpreted by the client in a way that is best suited to them.

Whether someone actually is terminal is a whole chapter in itself which is out of scope for this piece of work. Let's just say that doctors very often get this wrong. With this in mind, I suspect statements such as the following may be effective for some people:

"I may live far longer than anyone imagined!"

"I've got this!"

"I am going to smash this illness"

This last sentence includes a useful power word - "smash" that for many really ramps up the power of whatever is being said. This, along with, "I've got this" both adopt the attitude of defiance and conquering against all odds. I can only imagine that his would benefit many people in this scenario.

Fear of Death

Many of us don't dwell too much on the idea of death. However, for some people, this concept is particularly emotionally charged. Some will have a particular image, scene or idea in mind that simply needs to be Click Tracked. However, this area in particular is one in which the emotion removal tracks such as the EEF and Click Track 2015 can be a bit hit or miss in my experience.

Mr C

This case study is a perfect one to illustrate each of the steps taken when things don't go smoothly. Mr C had intense emotion when even the topic of death got brought up. In fact he would literally burst into tears if the word death was uttered.

Each of the steps that follow could have solved the problem for someone else depending on how the problem is structured in their model of reality. I framed the process as an experimental one as usual to gain information about the nature of the issue, with the knowledge that emotional charge around the idea of death is one that can require more sophisticated work.

Because he could easily access the state at will, I had him do so and we ran a standard Click Track and an EEF on the emotion produced. This resulted in zero change and he actually had to stop midway through the EEF as it was too overwhelming. Therefore we needed to do some investigating.

It turns out the problem started when his uncle died 5 years previously. The memory of this brought up an upset of 7/10. I found the fact that this rating was lower than the concept of death alone strange because it both involves the problem concept as well as the memory of losing a loved one. I suspect the distance in time from the event played some role in this.

I framed the removal of grief as described earlier in this chapter and 2 EEF's later he felt completely calm about the memory of his uncle. I suspected that this would have undone the rest of the emotional turmoil, but the moment he thought about the idea of death again, he became very upset once more.

He wasn't entirely sure about why he was so emotive around this idea but, through conversation, it became clear that he had a background belief that his parents were going to die very soon. His parents were healthy and active and he had no reason to believe this would be the case. I toyed with the idea of applying a PSTEC Negative to this belief but any mention of the word death or words revolving around this idea brought instant and intense upset and he wasn't capable of doing any tracks whilst experiencing such feelings of overwhelm.

At this point, I suspected that to be successful we needed to come up with some PSTEC Positive statements that really resonated with him. This took some real digging around his model of reality and lots of trial and error to come up with a statement which resonated and didn't bring up any upset. During conversation it became apparent that the concepts that needed to be ramped up in his model of reality were "happy", "family", "together", "forever". This was the final sentence:

"My family and I are always going to be happy together".

This construction did the job and he felt calmness wash over him even after just saying it out loud and was able to say the word "death" out loud without upset. However, he was doubtful that this would last. Like others who express such a doubt, I advise keeping an open mind to avoid the risk of recreating a problem through scepticism and doubt, which has already been cleared. A month later he told me that he was sleeping ok and feeling calm and happy once more.

The important take away from this case study is the process and thinking that led to this final result. For example, this PSTEC Positive statement might work for some people but it was created specifically for his model of reality and was constructed through trial and error, conversation and by saying it out loud to test it was a good fit.

For a personal consultation visit: www.themindhealer.co.uk

Summary

As can be seen through the above case studies, dealing with grief is a bit of a minefield with a great variety of methods, techniques and approaches that can be employed and tested in various circumstances. It is a particularly good topic to highlight the framework set out in the introduction actually in action. I hope that the above has given you food for thought and ideas to either help yourself if you have lost a loved one, or to help your clients if you are a therapist. Perhaps, equally important, give some thought to how some of these approaches can be altered slightly to deal with a variety of different problems which may not be cleared by the basic Click Track approach or challenging thoughts alone.

For a personal consultation visit: www.themindhealer.co.uk

Anxiety, Depression, Suicidal Thoughts and Related Issues

This is a huge field which covers many psychological ailments. Moreover, these niggles often come packaged together. For example many of those who suffer from anxiety also suffer from depression and within the "anxiety" umbrella itself are a whole host of subdivisions, such as social anxiety and phobias. I am going to bombard with you lots of case studies which will reinforce the framework I have already set out and also be different enough from each other that you should be able to pick out specific nuances from each.

The first case study I describe is a great example of someone using the emotion clearing Click Tracks in conjunction with tasks.

Miss D - Tasks, YouTube and Systematic Desensitisation

Miss D was around 60 years old and had suffered greatly from anxiety, depression and panic attacks throughout her life. She had spent well over £20,000 over the years on therapy but nothing so far had worked. Her father was very aggressive and made her

For a personal consultation visit: www.themindhealer.co.uk

childhood very difficult through his behaviour and how he made her feel. She didn't realise it at the time but he was actually mentally ill and, as an adult looking back, there was no anger or resentment. In fact she actually felt sorry for him more than anything else.

In gathering information about a client's life, in a sense I am aiming for waking regression. In hypnotic regression, hypnosis is used to gain access to historical events which may be causally linked to the current problem. Almost all of my private client work is done over the phone or Skype and so I wanted some of the benefit that regression offers without requiring hypnosis to be carried out.

To aid me in this task, I aim to get my client to feel emotions as soon as possible. Rather than ask them to go for the earliest memory straight away, depending how old they are, I ask if anything painful had happened in the last 10 years. For teenagers I would normally ask whether they were in secondary school (aged 11-16), primary (7-11) or infant school (4-7).

I have them dive into the experience unless it is very traumatic. I ask them how they felt, where they were, who they were with, where they feel the emotion etc. I have them do the same with each event they describe, so not only am I gaining information but we also have an idea as to how much emotion is trapped within each event. Equally important is that in this emotional frame of mind, recall of other events within the same emotional sphere becomes much more likely. This has been proven countless times by psychologists and on a daily basis I unearth a

For a personal consultation visit: www.themindhealer.co.uk

client's hidden memories in this manner which would otherwise have remained repressed. Self-helpers can mimic this by writing out a timeline and really going into any emotions that are felt, right back to the age of 0-5 years old.

This lady was unusual in the sense that most of her trauma had occurred aged between 0-15 years old but none of it elicited any emotions. The years that followed up until present day were pretty uneventful in terms of additional life stressors, though the constant anxiety was bad enough. One option I had was to have her say out loud, "I had a very happy and carefree childhood" which may have brought up some emotion if any had been there due to it being a falsehood. Saying a statement like this, which is untrue, can often bring forth feelings which might otherwise be repressed. Having done so in this instance, it brought up nothing in addition to the constant anxiety she felt. In her head she thought that she could barely function in day to day life and that she had a mountain to climb.

It is very common for someone to feel like this when they have had so much anxiety for so long. However, I suggested that we write down the specific triggers which turned out to be:

Fear of hospitals
Fear of crowds
Fear of being in unfamiliar places alone
Fear of aggressive men

Although it was quite easy to avoid these triggers in day to day life, the fear from the thought of them was always at the back of

For a personal consultation visit: www.themindhealer.co.uk

her mind and kept her in a constant state of anxiety. I asked if she agreed that in a sense the problem would be non-existent if we cleared the anxiety related to these four things to which she agreed.

I asked if she would be willing to prove to herself that each of these issues had gone as we moved along by carrying out tasks. She was desperate for this lifelong problem to be gone and said she was up for anything. We then proceeded through a program of systematic desensitisation enhanced through PSTEC. This is a common psychological technique of gradually exposing a person to their fear. For example, someone scared of spiders may initially stare at a picture of a small one until their brain has become desensitised to it. Next they would progress to a picture of a bigger one or a video of one, all the way up to actually holding one.

In its traditional form, this is quite brutal and involves a lot of emotional pain for the person going through it. PSTEC makes the process far less brutal and much quicker. So in this instance I had her just imagine she was about to go to hospital and this brought up 10/10 anxiety. She Click Tracked this twice which brought the anxiety down to zero.

Her most vivid fear was being in a particular department within the hospital which puts her in complete meltdown. A specific memory was the cause of this but, oddly, the memory held no emotional content, whereas the scenario itself did so we focused on this. Always head in the direction their model of reality/subconscious mind is guiding us.

- 104 -

I next advised her that we would be splitting up the task of sitting down in that specific department into chunks. These would be driving to the hospital and parking up, standing in reception, heading towards the problem department and finally spending some time there to prove to herself that the fear really had gone.

Depending on the situation, I often have clients do a Click Track in the problem environment. It is best to be sat with eyes closed typically. However playing the track on your phone with headphones in, eyes open and going about your day also works (so long as it is safe to do so). People often feel embarrassed at this thought but a quick reframe squashes that. I tell them that they can tap with just one finger against their palm or thumb and that to imagine they are just tapping along to music.

Miss D had removed all fear at the thought of hospitals and so began driving to the hospital and parked up, at which point she felt zero fear. Next she walked into the reception of the hospital and a 5/10 anxiety came up which was removed with one Click Track. Next she headed over to the "problem" department and sat down. Normally at this point she would be in full blown panic but her anxiety was a more manageable 7/10 which was removed with two Click Tracks. She felt at this point that her fear of hospitals was done and dusted.

Next I suggested she tackle the fear of crowds and being in an unfamiliar place alone in one go. She chose a nearby city with which she was largely unfamiliar and had her husband drop her

For a personal consultation visit: www.themindhealer.co.uk

off and return a few hours later. There was also a carnival going on at the same time which of course meant huge crowds. Using the same procedure as last time, she broke up the task into chunks, starting off with clearing any emotion linked to the thought of it, then again the moment she was dropped off. Next she headed towards the crowds but by this point her anxiety had gone already, suggesting that crowds and unfamiliar places were linked conceptually within her model of reality.

A slightly trickier problem to deal with was anxiety towards aggressive men. It was more a case of anything that could be construed as confrontation rather than aggression, she admitted. Although it is normal for the heart rate to increase a little whilst in a confrontation, she experienced panic attacks if she observed the slightest disagreement between other people if one of them was a man. For some reason her response was more reasonable if women were involved.

We couldn't really use the same process we used for the previous problems with this one. We considered having her husband shout at her but she just laughed at this and said it wouldn't work. I asked her to look on YouTube and search for fights or arguments between men. There were thousands of these and watching them elicited the problem response.

I had her stare at the video whilst going through the Click Track. A few Click Tracks later and she felt completely calm no matter what she watched. There were particular situations at work which often triggered these feelings and she emailed a few weeks later

For a personal consultation visit: www.themindhealer.co.uk

to say that the usual triggers were having no impact on her any more.

At the time I carried out this session, PSTEC Negative and Click Track 2015 didn't exist. If they had I may have considered utilising them in combination with PSTEC Positive, the standard Click Track and EEF's which may have shortened the time taken to clear the emotion in the problem contexts. However she was responding so well to the tracks we were using that, even now, I may have continued pursuing this approach.

I think this is a useful case study to describe because it introduces the idea of systematic desensitisation, using tasks to further cement the work and also using something like YouTube to initiate the problem response which is difficult to bring up otherwise.

Mr T - suicidal thoughts, anxiety and severe depression

Remember the boy who wasn't allowed above ground floor through fears he may jump out of the window? It then became apparent that he was using words such as suicide as an expression of how much he was struggling rather than any real intent to end his life. His problem is a very interesting one which doesn't follow the usual route and so should be valuable to see how I dealt with it.

There was a brief period of bullying a few years previously which had no emotional charge now and he said it wasn't such a big deal at the time because it got dealt with straight away. Other than this there didn't appear to be any outward reason for the way he felt and he said that he had been like this for all of his life. I checked on with how things were in different parts of his life but his home and school life seemed healthy on the surface.

I asked him to think back and describe the earliest memory he had of feeling this way. Prior to this I had asked him to describe in detail how he was feeling and had him delve right into it to increase the chance that we hit upon a relevant memory. Within seconds an image of him came up being all alone in nursery and about a 7/10 upset came up. This is a very common early memory that crops up for many people I have worked with.

He agreed it might help if we cleared the emotion with a Click Track. In most cases like these with such a distant and early memory that is so vague, the emotion is cleared very quickly as well as any beliefs which link to it. In this instance a few Click Tracks didn't budge it one bit. Through the tracks he didn't appear to be concentrating and was looking around despite reminders that he needs to concentrate. Sometimes people with ADHD and younger children can inadvertently do this with without meaning to.

In this instance I sensed subconscious sabotage. To test this I had him say out loud: "I deserve to be happy" to see if any resistance popped up. He said this and had a clear emotional response to his surprise. It is quite common for these kinds of beliefs to be hidden from the person who holds them in their model of reality.

For a personal consultation visit: www.themindhealer.co.uk

By this point he had already been informed about the nature of beliefs and thought. He agreed that he did want to get better, even though a part of him didn't think he deserved it. This served as useful introduction to the idea that we all consist of different parts, to help him further dissociate himself from his model of reality. We had a quick chat about his thoughts and feelings and it seemed as though he believed the following: "I have the belief that I am bad".

He agreed to run a PSTEC Negative on this belief. We spent a little time talking about how the opposite is true and then ran the track. I have been down this route many times with clients and most of the time a PSTEC Negative on a belief like this quickly unravels it. However, straight after he said he didn't think it had made a difference, but his model of reality had offered him a little more information in the form of adding a word to the end of the belief: "I have the belief that I am bad for being alive". This shed a little light on why the word suicide was being used, even though he had no intention of this.

The first time that he had indicated to the school that he was intending to jump out of the window, a crisis team was called. He was taken to Accident and Emergency where he stayed for the night before coming home. Following my initial chat with him I let him know that I was going to inform the school about what he had really meant when he said he was suicidal and wanted to jump out of the window. He was ok with this as I had explained how worried everyone had been, and he was ok with school checking if he meant it literally before taking action in future.

For a personal consultation visit: www.themindhealer.co.uk

A few days after my initial brief chat with him, during which I found out what he really meant, he made the same threats again at school. However this time the school asked if he wanted them to call the hospital again and if he wanted to spend another night there. They called his bluff and he said that he would rather they didn't and off he went to class. If he did mean it literally, the school of course would have taken the necessary steps to keep him safe.

At this point what would be your next step if you were with this client or working on yourself? Before moving on, please pause for a few moments and think about it. When ready turn the page to find out what I did next.

Mr T - Continued

When working on yourself or other people I think it is a good idea to come up with potential theories as these can give you a bit of a pathway to move forward. It doesn't matter if there is no way of ever proving/disproving the theory.

I thought that one possibility was that maybe there was secondary gain to be had here with all the attention that using words like "suicide" can generate. If this was the case, maybe the actual problem was one in which he didn't feel loved or just needed a little more attention than he was currently getting.

However, although there may have been a small element of this involved, I sensed that his response to the previous tracks that

For a personal consultation visit: www.themindhealer.co.uk

we worked on rendered other explanations more likely, so I decided to head down that route.

The next question I pondered is why he wasn't responding to the tracks. Most people do, but you do occasionally get someone for whom they don't resonate. Also, he seemed to be looking around a lot through the track so he may have had some problems with focusing. Another explanation is that this could have been part of the subconscious sabotage.

I decided to go down the route of focusing on the belief that he was bad for being alive and use conversation within the perspective of the model of reality which I had already explained to him. My plan was to rip apart his concept of "bad" and alter his thinking in this realm. I first asked him when this belief was born. The idea of a belief being born is quite a strange one and presupposes that it wasn't there from birth. He said that it was born when he was aged 2-3 years old.

I explained that, as we go through life, we come to many conclusions and adopt many beliefs that, years later, can seem quite ridiculous. For example, if I told him there was a monster under the table, he wouldn't likely be scared. However if a 3 year old's belief in monsters stuck in place well into adulthood, then I could very easily scare that person simply by the suggestion that I just saw a monster under the table.

I asked him if he could take seriously a belief and conclusion that he came to when he was 2-3 years old and maybe only just learned to walk. He laughed and said maybe not. I next asked if

For a personal consultation visit: www.themindhealer.co.uk

he had been "bad" today. He thought long and hard and replied "No". I asked the same question about yesterday, last week and so on and he said that the last time he had been bad, he had been angry at his sister about three weeks ago.

It then became clear that if he ever expressed anger, it meant that he was a bad person in his mind. In other words very black and white, rigid thinking which we also had to dismantle. I asked if he chose to be angry in that scenario and he said that he didn't and that it just happened automatically. I suggested that he was coming to the conclusion that he was a bad person for something that is completely out of his control.

For those familiar with my work on characters in PSTEC Advanced Part 2, this was his inner Judge at work. When we notice a rule that the Judge is holding, it is a good idea to analyse it from different perspectives. First we see if that rule applies to other people and I checked if his sister ever gets angry with him and that, if so, is she a bad person? I also asked if he thought a brother and sister had ever existed in the history of humanity who hadn't at some point become angry with each other? He laughed and agreed that the answer was probably no.

It is always a very powerful moment when I can get a person to laugh at a particular problem structure within their model of reality and a key way to do this is to take the thought/belief/rule, expand it and apply it to different scenarios, as we have done here. This very often is enough to pop that reality tunnel.

For a personal consultation visit: www.themindhealer.co.uk

There was still an active feature of his thinking that led him to believe that if he was bad once that meant he was a bad person. The previous conversation had obviously had an impact on his physiology but a little more work was required. To break down this rigidity we co-constructed a PSTEC Positive statement which broke the idea of badness from the identity level to the day to day level.

There are some people for who only conversation and PSTEC Positive seems to have any impact and I sensed this was the case here, given the lack of result from the previous work, and this is why I didn't revisit PSTEC Negative at this point. The statement we tested and worked with was: "Today I am going to be a good person". Prior to this we attempted a more ambitious identity level change of "I really am a good person" but it was too far removed from his model of reality as it currently existed, and his model of reality gave feedback to indicate this in that it just didn't resonate or feel real for him. After running the finalised thought through PSTEC Positive he felt completely calm with all distress gone.

I saw him again two weeks later. He said that he felt great until two days ago when the thought that he was a bad person came back. The trigger was a boy in school barging into him in the corridor. He felt anger and threw an empty plastic bottle at the lad. The fact that the old belief came back just meant that we had more work to do to solidify the new ways of thinking within his model of reality.

For a personal consultation visit: www.themindhealer.co.uk

I explained the evolutionary need for anger and that his brain quite rightly felt under attack. I also explained that most people would feel anger in that scenario. He told me that although he felt like a bad person again it wasn't as severe as before. The statement of "Today I am going to be a good person" still resonated most and one run through of that left him calm and more accepting towards himself again. If a person's model of reality rejects an idea on one occasion, it doesn't mean that it will reject it forever so I had him say out the identity level statement of "I am a good person" and this time it really resonated. I saw this as definite evidence that changes were being made in the right direction. We played around with the wording to see if we could ramp up the power of the statement further before running the track and the final statement we ended on was: "I really am a good person" - with the word "really" having quite a big boosting effect. This is always a useful word to test within a PSTEC Positive statement to see if it can make the statement seem more powerful.

We ran through the statement a few times and he really felt great afterwards. More work was required moving forward on other things but this was the key breakthrough.

Miss G – self-hate, suicidal thoughts and use of the Accelerator

My client had told me via email that she was severely depressed. However when she came on Skype she was hysterically upset and in the background I could see a noose, which she told me was ready in case I couldn't help as she just couldn't take it anymore.

For a personal consultation visit: www.themindhealer.co.uk

She had already been through mainstream psychological routes in America to no avail, so she clearly needed an alternative approach and was unwilling to contact emergency services in what actually was an emergency.

She had all of the PSTEC products but had only used the basic Click Tracks which hadn't helped her. It became clear quite early on that major subconscious resistance to getting better was in play. I determined this through her excessive use of "yes but" to almost anything I suggested without giving it any real thought or consideration. Any Click Tracks we used on current minor stressors made no impact.

I told her that she obviously wanted to feel better otherwise she wouldn't have contacted me, but that I suspect that a part of her may not feel like she deserves to feel better or that it is safe to do so. I explained that is very common and to test this I asked her to say out loud:

"I deserve to be happy".

She attempted to say it but before a word was uttered she burst into tears. I asked if she hated herself to which she said "yes" over and over. Another key sentence I ask people to say out loud is "It is safe to feel happy" or "It is safe to feel safe". An emotional response/resistance to either of these questions points to where further work is required to undo the sabotage.

At the time this took place, PSTEC Negative wasn't around so that wasn't a potential path to go down. I attempted to determine how long this self-hate had been there but she had zero memory of her childhood. Whenever this is the case, I see red warning flags that there may be painful memories that are being repressed. Some people just have bad memory with nothing more sinister than that but with a combination of self-hate and intense emotional pain, I suspected that that is where the problem lay.

I had her focus on her self-hate and run through an Accelerator track in the hope that a causal memory may crop up (The PSTEC Accelerator tracks can expose causal memories as well is turn down the feeling). During the first run through, a definite age of 9 years old popped into her mind but nothing more. We ran it again and again and each time more information came up; first the location, then who was present, then finally what was happening. She had been raped by her uncle and the memory had been completely repressed ever since. She was very emotional, but knowing the cause was cathartic for her. Many children who are abused often blame themselves and as a result hate themselves. In fact this happens in almost every case I have worked on of this nature (which sadly is many) and even as adults, they know logically that it wasn't their fault but the feeling remains as though it is.

With the "cat out of the bag" we set about running the EEF's on the emotion linked to it. This time with full awareness of the cause, the subconscious mind offered no resistance and it only took one listen to remove all pain from this incident. The feeling of relief was immense for this person and the many current issues which beforehand had been very emotionally charged, disappeared of their own accord. No further work was required.

- 116 -

Sometimes when an issue is completely tied up within one traumatic event from the distant past, simply clearing the emotion linked to it can be enough to set everything back to peace and calm.

Miss B - sex trafficking victim

There is a lot of badness in the world. However, I cannot think of a more vile crime than sex trafficking and I am sure that one day I will play a role in somehow making the PSTEC suite of tools available to these poor people to ease their suffering.

Miss B had escaped her situation 2 years previously but was still severely traumatised. It was a very complex case and I am going to focus on just a few of the more important things we worked on which will serve to further illustrate principles already described. Click Track 2015 was a key component of this work with its emphasis on safety and letting go of bad feelings amongst the suggestions on the track; the two things which she really needed.

In terms of releasing emotions, she did respond well to the likes of the EEF when we focused on individual traumas, but a key breakthrough came when we ran the long Click Track 2015, which is about 28 minutes long. This cleansed her emotionally of the years of trauma she had been through.

What I want to focus on here is her self image. When she looked into a mirror she saw an ugly face covered in spots and blemishes. When she initially told me this, I assumed that she might have been interpreting natural variations in skin colour we all have as something more. However I think anyone else would agree she had smooth skin and would be considered attractive by most standards.

With the more complex cases I like to compile a belief bucket in which we identify a few beliefs and brainstorm ideas of what else might be in there. I will often begin to make suggestions of beliefs which I suspect will probably be held within their model of reality based on our conversations and then we expand on this.

This brought up beliefs such as the following:

- I am not attractive
- People will reject me
- I am an outcast
- People judge me badly
- Kind people are weak people
- If people like me I will be abused

Some of these beliefs she was unaware of before we went through this process. She had a huge amount of self-hate with the way she looked. She agreed that it might be better if she felt more at peace about the way she looked regardless of how good or bad she thought she looked. We began with a Click Track whilst visualising herself to activate the self-hate.

She felt calmer after this but still believed she was ugly. We ran a PSTEC Negative on "I have the belief that I am ugly". Halfway through, she jumped out of her chair having a major panic attack and I took this reaction as subconscious resistance to letting go of that belief.

To test this, once the panic had subsided I had her say out loud, "It is safe to feel attractive" and she was unable to say it. Considering what she had been through as well as this response, I guessed that the problem belief was something along the lines of "If I am attractive I will be abused" or "If I am attractive I am in danger". This belief felt true for her and so we proceeded.

She was already well aware of how the mind worked and I put forth the theory that given what she had been through, it makes sense that the belief had become active in her model of reality, especially at that time in her life as she was in a very vulnerable position. In other words, it may have served a useful purpose at that point in time. I then went on to explain that sometimes a belief passes it sell by date and that in this instance, taking into account that her situation is far safer, the chance of a repeat was extremely slim given her much more stable situation at home.

She agreed that this made sense and agreed to try a PSTEC Negative on "I have the belief that if I am attractive, I am in danger". This had a calming impact and we tested the work by having her say out loud again, "It is safe to feel attractive". This time there was no emotional resistance.

Next I suggested that we leave out the concept of attractive/unattractive and come up with a statement which allowed her to feel at peace with how she looked. She agreed and we tested a few out and this one resonated the most, "From now

For a personal consultation visit: www.themindhealer.co.uk

on I can feel safe and at peace with how I look". She felt even more relaxed after this and went to the toilet. When she came back she looked in total shock. When she looked in the mirror whilst washing her hands her appearance had changed beyond recognition.

She really had been seeing a disfigured face full of scars, spots and blemishes and now what she saw was her face and skin as smooth and flawless for the first time. I theorised that the trauma had been so severe that her brain had created a representation of her face which made her feel as though she was ugly and therefore would be less likely to be abused. Although, in doing this, her model of reality created a lot of self-hate, at least she was able to feel a little safer. I suspect talking therapy alone may struggle to achieve this kind of result so quickly and it's another demonstration of the fact that we don't experience reality directly, but instead, our experience is constructed by our models of reality through the filters of our beliefs and knowledge.

Miss Y - rape and court case

Earlier I described a girl who felt that she was trapped in a dark place and felt much better after running a PSTEC Negative on this idea. This is what happened in the year leading up to that point. When I first saw her she was very volatile emotionally. She had been raped 6 months previously and the attacker had been caught. Since then she had major mood swings from anger to upset with the core background emotion of anxiety. Thinking of the trauma itself left her feeling sick but not completely overwhelmed. People respond to trauma in different ways and I

For a personal consultation visit: www.themindhealer.co.uk

would normally take a gentler approach but her lack of overwhelm lead me to experiment trying an EEF track directly on the event. Two listens left her feeling completely calm to her amazement. In fact she was buzzing because the contrast between how she was feeling compared to how she felt straight after the track was huge and felt like a massive burden had been lifted.

She was at school and so it was easy to keep tabs on how she was doing. She had been fine for three weeks until the attacker began sending her death threats and stalking her. This had instigated nightmares every night and she was in a constant state of panic. She agreed that, despite everything, she would be better off without the anxiety and that it was just making her miserable.

Even though she had responded so well to the Click Track last time, I decided we needed to talk a little about the danger before removing the anxiety. Apparently, the attacker was tagged and so the police were aware of his whereabouts. She agreed that so long as she ensured that she was always with other people until the court case, it was very unlikely that anything would happen. She also decided to buy a rape/attack alarm so she could at least alert people in the unlikely event that anything did happen. The police had also already given her safety advice which she was happy to follow.

This conversation alone left her feeling calmer and one Click Track left her feeling relaxed. I explained that we can use our imagination to torture ourselves or to feel better and it made more sense to use it for the latter. The PSTEC Positive statement

For a personal consultation visit: www.themindhealer.co.uk

of "Everything is going to be ok" resonated with her and she felt good afterwards. Thankfully she had no further run-ins with the attacker and therefore felt calm for the next 5 months.

The anxiety returned as the court case was approaching. You might imagine that the anxiety might be about seeing her attacker again but I never make any assumptions. It turned out that she had dyslexia and was very nervous about a part of the court proceedings in which she had to read out an oath. We figured out what she would have to say and had her do some practicing. Next we ran a PSTEC Positive on "I shall feel calm and confident whilst reading the oath at court". The response to this was unexpected but also endearing. She began jumping up and down excitedly saying, "I can't believe it! I can't believe it! I feel ok now!" Although a little nervous on the day, she managed to get through it far better than she would have thought before our work with PSTEC and she managed to read the oath perfectly.

Mr S - social anxiety and the fear of being judged

Mr S had suffered from severe social anxiety all of his life. To complicate matters he was going through the process of a sex change. Identity level change can be very unsettling for anyone and I imagine even more so for those who undergo a physical transformation such as Mr S was doing.

His social anxiety possibly stemmed from the fact that for most of his life he felt like a man trapped in a woman's body. Regardless, it was my job to enable him to feel more at peace in himself. Through conversation it became apparent that his main concern was fear of being judged.

For a personal consultation visit: www.themindhealer.co.uk

Prior to this I had trawled through his life history with nothing of note to be seen which may be contributing to his current anxiety beyond his thinking. Fear of being judged is extremely common in many people. From a survival and evolutionary perspective, thousands of years ago we literally needed our tribe. If we were rejected by our tribe we would literally not last very long out in the wild alone. Therefore it makes sense why people fear rejection so much, even though rejection isn't likely to lead to death these days.

Lots of anxiety and upset came up at the thought of being judged. If emotion spontaneously comes up like this I will often begin with a Click Track to see if we can clear it, even if the issue seems to be directly belief related. It went from an 8/10 all the way down after to zero after one listen. I asked him to think about being judged to see if he could bring any back and the emotion came back instantly.

I could have played a few more emotion removing Click Tracks but I sensed that making a change at the belief and viewpoint level would be of more benefit at this point. I explained why the fear of being judged is hardwired into us and delved further into this particular structure within his model of reality. Corresponding beliefs of being rejected and not being worthy if he was rejected came up. I also explained that there appeared to be a background belief that we actually are what other people think of us.

For a personal consultation visit: www.themindhealer.co.uk

We analysed the concept of being judged and rejected. What does it actually mean to be judged? People's brains automatically form opinions the moment we meet someone. For many people these opinions may form and then they go back to worrying about themselves for the rest of the day. The opinions also have little to do with actual reality. They are merely a by-product of how that person's model of reality is constructed, which is largely a result of their random life experiences.

I told him to imagine that he was going to meet fifty new people over the coming week and each would get to know him very well. I asked if he felt that each would have the same opinion of him or would they each probably have very different views. He agreed that they each would probably have their own take on him and his situation. Next I asked if other people's opinion had any actual bearing on whom he is as a person? If so, how would he choose which people to choose to believe as they couldn't all be right. I also pointed out that even the opinion of one person is prone to change from moment to moment, so would that mean that he would become a different person from moment to moment also?

Once we had deconstructed these ideas on being judged and what it actually means, we began on the concept of rejection. What does rejection actually mean? In his model of reality it turned out that it meant that some people might have a negative opinion of him.

I asked him if he thought there was a person alive who doesn't have someone who has a negative opinion of them? When

For a personal consultation visit: www.themindhealer.co.uk

deconstructing concepts which are problematic for someone it is a good idea to take them to extremes like this as their falsehood often becomes much easier to see.

I next offered a differing viewpoint which might be more useful. I suggested that as we go through life we all meet many people, some of whom we are a good fit with and others less so. We tend to spend more time with people we gel with and less with those that we don't. When we don't gel with someone, all it means is that the random construction of ours and their model of reality aren't quite matched. It doesn't mean that they are bad, it is their fault or vice versa. It's a little like two people having a different favourite colour; after all we don't consciously choose which colours will be more appealing to us more than others.

He agreed all of this makes sense and he said he had never thought of it like that before. Next we applied this new framework onto his current situation. I suggested that if someone has a problem with his transgender status, that rather than meaning anything about him as a person, it is really just a reflection of their model of reality. In other words it is just "data" being gathered about the other person and if what they say is negative, then it is providing useful information that they probably wouldn't be a good fit friendship wise and not to invest much time or energy into them.

It is such a powerful procedure to have someone dissociate from their thinking in this way and try on new perspectives to see how they fit. The next step in the framework was to identify positive resources in his model of reality. He actually had a very close

For a personal consultation visit: www.themindhealer.co.uk

social group of family and friends who were all very supportive and he felt loved by them. This was useful information we utilised in PSTEC Positive statements.

We tested out various potential statements to reinforce the above ideas and the first one we went for based on how it felt was:

"I am a good person regardless what people think"

Following this we were able to ramp up the feeling by adding the concept of safety to the mix:

"I am safe whether people judge me or not"

Finally we ended with:

"I am always going to be supported by people close to me".

This trio of new beliefs left Mr S feeling great. He thought about the idea of people judging him and he just laughed and said, "It doesn't matter, if they are the kind of people who judge me, then their opinion isn't very important to me." This response represented a huge shift in thinking. It wasn't an intellectual conclusion but more of a true knowing.

I am a huge fan of James Tripp and I first came across the following distinction through him. He explains that in ancient Greece they had two different words for two types of knowledge. Eiden represents intellectual understanding and Gnosis represents experiential and operational understanding.

A very common area that this is especially relevant for, is that of people who hate themselves. Some people can list reasons why they deserve their self-hate but many actually have no idea why they hate themselves. They can understand completely from an intellectual, or "eiden" perspective that they perhaps don't deserve this self-punishment, but this alone often isn't enough to change their experience in life to that of one who doesn't hate themselves.

I always strive to head for gnosis of the new understanding. Sometimes this can be achieved through bypassing subconscious resistance and breaking down concepts and offering alternative viewpoints. What makes PSTEC so powerful, useful and different to any other therapeutic modality is how quickly you can go from Eiden to Gnosis through the Click Tracks and Belief Change tracks.

This is just one example of a client obtaining a new intellectual understanding but it required the PSTEC Positive tracks to push it towards gnosis so it not only made sense but felt true too.

Miss H - social anxiety and the use of tasks and skill acquisition

People suffering from social anxiety often demonstrate similar patterns of thinking and so similar solutions can be applied. However, each situation is unique and this case shows how some additional solutions helped to solidify the change.

For a personal consultation visit: www.themindhealer.co.uk

Miss H was a painfully shy schoolgirl and I had to spend a lot of time rapport building and helping her to feel comfortable with me. Last summer her house had been burgled whilst she had been on holiday with her parents. Ever since then she had been in a state of very high anxiety at all times.

She managed to tell me about what happened and also that her parents had since fitted CCTV and an alarm. As usual I presented the nature of thought and reality to get her to a point in which she agrees that it would be useful to try on different perspectives. She acknowledged that with the added security the chance of her house being burgled is massively reduced and that it makes more sense to use her imagination to feel calm and safe rather than worried all of the time.

We ran a Click Track on the memory of when they first found their house burgled which worked very well and was followed by a PSTEC Positive statement of "No matter what happens, everything is going to be ok". Afterwards she felt no anxiety about that memory or the thought of being burgled.

The reason I tackled this before dealing with her social anxiety is because the latter often requires a little more work and restructuring within the model of reality. Clearing the first trauma would not only familiarise her with the power of a tool such as PSTEC but also prevent that particular issue getting in the way of progress we make on the social anxiety front.

In her case she had a specific fear of and belief that she would be rejected. Unlike the last case described, there didn't seem to be

For a personal consultation visit: www.themindhealer.co.uk

any worry about what people thought of her. I deconstructed the idea as I did with Mr S, encouraging the notion that in life there are some people we are a good fit with and some we aren't. This new information alone seemed to make a big difference, to such an extent that it didn't appear as though any additional work was required to move it from an intellectual understanding to an operational feeling of its truth.

However, there was still big sticking point which was holding things back. Miss H simply didn't know what to say and how to even initiate a conversation. There are certain situations like this in which skill acquisition is required in addition to removing as much belief and emotional barriers to change.

She was in the first year of secondary school (aged 12) and although having been there for 6 months hadn't really had a conversation with any of the other pupils. However in my search for any hidden resources she already possessed, I found out that she was actually an excellent musician and who regularly performed in front of 100's of people. I utilised this to make her realise how amazing she was and also the fact that many people feel dread at the mere thought of any kind of performing, yet there she was doing it each week without any shred of anxiety.

In addition to boosting her self-esteem, I wanted to use this to help dissociate her from her current reality tunnel. I explained that "her brain" had come to the conclusion that it is safe to perform in front of many people but not safe talking to people, and we just need to teach it that she was safe in both scenarios.

For a personal consultation visit: www.themindhealer.co.uk

I explained we needed to teach it by carrying out a few tasks. We identified three people who she felt relatively comfortable with and then out of the three chose one that she would initiate a conversation with. She chose one who was also a musician and then we came up with exactly what to say. This was something along the lines of asking how her weekend had gone and if she had practiced her music much.

We actually came up with a few potential things to say and she felt most comfortable with the ones just mentioned. We decided on when she was going to initiate the conversation (which just happened to be immediately after the session as it was break time) and I also checked in with her to see if she could think of potential obstacles to her just doing it. When it comes to tasks I always do this and if anything does crop up we form a solution there and then before the task takes place. You shall see more examples of this as we progress. In this case she couldn't think of any reason why she wouldn't do it. I think because she knew exactly what she was going to say and that the worse-case scenario was that the conversation didn't continue and she felt quite calm. If there had been any anxiety at this point I may have ran a Click Track and created some PSTEC Positive statements but this wasn't necessary on this occasion.

In these kinds of scenarios I also present a very useful way of thinking of anxiety if any does come up. I advise thinking of it as a much younger part of you which is scared and just needs some reassurance from you to tell it that everything will be ok. Many people find this a useful frame to work with.

I saw her two weeks later with a background plan to create some more tasks and maybe teach her some conversation skills. However this wasn't necessary; the conversation she had went very well, she had formed two new friends who had since been around to her house. She had literally never had any friends over to her house prior to this so her mother was thrilled. I believe that if I had given her the task of "making new friends" without the specifics to begin with, she wouldn't have made the progress she did.

We did a little further work moving forward but the bulk of the change occurred in that first session. We have some very powerful tools to make changes to the model of reality, but we mustn't forget that experiences and action themselves can be powerful instigators of change to a person's model of reality. By taking action she received direct evidence that rejection wasn't a foregone conclusion and that after the initial conversation was started, she found it quite easy to talk to people.

Miss E - highly hypnotisable client

Miss E was an extremely able student and was suffering intense exam anxiety and in her mock exams experienced multiple panic attacks. She was easily able to bring up major anxiety at the thought of an exam two months away and listening to two Click Tracks removed it all. I even followed this up with a PSTEC Positive statement, "I am going to smash these exams" after which she was feeling very confident.

For a personal consultation visit: www.themindhealer.co.uk

Once I clear an emotion, I often have the client try to bring it back. Often they can't and if they can, it can just mean a little more work is required. In her case, it came back to a 10/10 within seconds. We ran another Click Track which again removed it completely and again it came back within seconds. She had led an uneventful and happy life and admitted that she can get herself wound up very easily. This led me to consider that she may be a highly hypnotisable client. In other words she may be someone who responds very well to therapy but can quite easily recreate a problem with her thoughts and self-talk compared to other people.

Once we had cleared the anxiety again and she was feeling calm and happy I gave her a task. I asked her to write down "I am going to smash these exams" twice a day; once before bed and first thing in the morning. She agreed to the task and the anxiety didn't come back at all.

Once you understand the quirks of your own or a client's model of reality, it is easy to design and implement a plan based on these unique features. I made her aware that negative thinking and suggestions have the power to undo the calmness and if she ever felt as if she was "going under" all she had to do was affirm the suggestions and this worked well for her.

Most people aren't highly hypnotisable in this sense and often if an emotion or problem comes back, more digging and additional work may be required.

Miss B - anxiety and gaining rapport in difficult situations

The problem of children refusing to go to school due to anxiety and other reasons is widespread. I chose this case study due to the unique challenge I faced when first beginning the session, as well as how I identified the cause and cleared the anxiety. It will further elucidate how I go about getting into their "castle" and self-helpers may benefit from the identification of an underlying cause.

In many cases we have the surface level anxiety but that is often just a symptom of a deeper level anxiety or upset about something else. Very often the person suffering is unaware of this deeper level. Miss B's anxiety was so bad that I had to visit her at her house. When I arrived she had locked herself in her bedroom and was refusing to come out.

I stood there for 20 minutes whilst her mother tried to persuade her to open the door but she just completely ignored her pleas. Finally she managed to force open the door and she was stood in the corner of the bathroom facing the wall and completely ignoring everything we said.

Like many other children I see, Miss B had seen many counsellors and therapists without much change in how she felt. Therefore my first aim is to indicate that I offer something different to other people who may have tried to help her in the past. However, it is a little tricky doing this with someone who is stood facing a wall, completely disengaged from you.

For a personal consultation visit: www.themindhealer.co.uk

I needed to input some information into her model of reality. In hypnosis there is a technique called "my friend John" in which you utilise a story about one of your other clients or someone you know who faced a particular problem. Often embedded within the story is a useful solution or way of thinking about the situation. Because the information is about someone else and their situation, the client's barriers are far lower and therefore much more likely to take on board the useful information passively. This kind of technique I use extensively with children in certain schools who have extreme behaviour problems and are very unresponsive to help generally speaking, and I shall talk in more detail about this later.

In this scenario I decided to draw on the advantages of the "my friend John" technique by applying the process to her mother. I basically ran a session with her mother, had her think of something that was bothering her, ran through my pre-talk and explanation which was all within the earshot of Miss B. She thought of a stressful event in her past and was about to follow the Click Track. Just before we were about to begin I made my first and only reference to Miss B and said that she may as well just play along and tap along whilst thinking about school or anything that is bothering her.

To reduce the risk of resistance as much as possible, I said that she could do it without us knowing (we couldn't see her hands) and that afterwards she still didn't have to speak to me. She ignored me and I went through the process with her mother a few times on different things. Her mother was genuinely amazed

For a personal consultation visit: www.themindhealer.co.uk

at the change she felt which would likely have had an impact on her daughter.

After this I explained to her where she could download the tracks if Miss B decided she would like to try them in her own time and I left without a word being spoken between us. Some of the schools I work in can only afford to have me once or twice a year and so it was about 3 months later that I went back to that school. Apparently Miss B had been tapping along and felt so much better during the time that I was sat on the floor outside her bedroom and as a result, cleared a lot of anxiety which led to her going back to school full time a week later.

When I saw her again she was laughing at her behaviour when I said it was nice to be speaking to the front of her face rather than the back of her head for a change. She said that although she was able to come into school now she did suffer with a lot of anxiety despite using the tracks at home.

A quick conversation about her past led to the cause. Her father had died quickly and unexpectedly when she was just 7 years old and she was flooded with intense upset at the memory. I gave my pre-frame of how to view situations like this as I described in detail in the chapter on grief and she agreed that it might be useful to clear it. One Click Track on this cleared all anxiety and upset linked to this event.

Imagine the impact of the death of a parent on a 7 year old. Her model of reality would likely have formed the belief that people you love and need can be taken without warning and so it is

For a personal consultation visit: www.themindhealer.co.uk

hardly surprisingly that along with the grief, she had been carrying around a lot of anxiety since that point. Perhaps it was anxiety that if she wasn't near her mother that she may leave as well, rather than any anxiety about school. I have found that fear of something happening to parents is a very common feature of those refusing to go to school.

In this instance it appeared that the Click Track removed both the emotion as well as the beliefs embedded within them as we didn't have to do any work on beliefs. I saw her again 6 months on and she was happy and enjoying school.

Miss J - agoraphobia

Miss J was also a "school refuser" but this was also developing into a deeper fear of leaving the home. It began suddenly and without warning a month ago without any obvious triggers. School was getting a bit more stressful but she was having full blown panic attacks at just the thought of going school and, more recently, leaving the house.

I always go for the simplest and quickest solution possible so had her think about school and then ran a Click Track on the 10/10 anxiety this produced. I ran a few of the more powerful emotion neutralising tracks and still no change. When there is no obvious trigger I delve into the past to hunt out historical pain, even if it seems unrelated. Three years previously she had lost a grandparent and this was still very painful for her.

For a personal consultation visit: www.themindhealer.co.uk

She recalled wanting to see the grandparent one particular day but she had to go to school and he died whilst she was at school. When very strong emotions are present it is easy for our models of reality to come up with beliefs and ideas which might seem bizarre and illogical to us when we are feeling calm. Intuitively, I asked if she felt any blame for what happened and a torrent of tears emerged and she nodded that yes, it was indeed her fault. She felt that if she had been able to see him he would have been alright.

We ran some Click Tracks on this pain and she felt much more at peace about that specific memory but she still blamed herself without really knowing why. Through conversation she realised that she held a belief that if she wasn't with her family, they were in danger. Coincidentally, quite recently her mother had picked up a bad cough which wasn't shifting at around the time that the severe anxieties about school began to emerge. Her mother soon got better but we concluded that if anyone held the belief that their family are in danger of becoming ill and dying if they weren't home, and then a family member developed a very bad cough, it makes sense that their subconscious mind might try to protect their family by discouraging them from going to school by creating anxiety.

There is always a beautiful logic hidden behind what appears to be quite bizarre on the surface. This theory seemed to really hit the nail on the head as she was gobsmacked that this did in fact "feel" right. With this knowledge we listed reasons why it might be better to let go of this way of thinking in order to prepare her model of reality for change. We ran a PSTEC Negative on "I

- 137 -

have the belief that my family are in danger without me". She felt calm and confused after this.

We tried out various potential PSTEC Positive statements and the one that resonated the most was a simple, "Everything is going to be ok". Whilst going through this she pictured going through school life completely calm and happy, whilst knowing that her family was safe.

Although working with a "school refuser" isn't something that crops up every day, I think this case study is a good one to include as it shows another example of how to dig deeper when the surface level procedures aren't achieving the desired results.

Mr G - suicidal with zero response to Click Tracks

Most people who feel suicidal respond very well to the PSTEC suite of tools. However, if they are completely physiologically and psychologically overwhelmed, shaking and struggling to focus on anything, they aren't always able to do a Click Track. If they can do a Click Track, the effort involved on top of their existing state is sometimes a bit too much and so other approaches might be required.

A few years ago Mr G phoned me out of the blue and was in a really bad way and scared of what he might do. He could barely speak and given the severity of the situation I advised him to phone the emergency services. However, he refused, saying that he had felt like this for the last 10 months and that every time he had phoned them, they had never been able to help. He had also tried numerous medications which always made him feel worse and the clinical psychologists he had seen hadn't been able to help either.

He downloaded a Click Track and although he was able to follow along with it just about, it was making no difference. I began finding out a little about his history and made some suggestions. However, each suggestion I made was instantly deflected without much thought, which points a finger towards some kind of subconscious sabotage. Some of my ideas were met with a "yes I've tried that before and it didn't work", yet when I asked what it was he had tried specifically, what he responded with had little resemblance to my suggestions.

I had him say out loud, "I deserve to be happy", which was met with definite emotional resistance. Normally in this kind of scenario a PSTEC Negative would be a good idea but in this case it wasn't possible. I also checked how he would feel doing a Belief Blaster on "I wasn't good enough". However he didn't want to do that because the past tense nature of it made him feel anxious given his suicidal state. I always check how a person feels about adding or removing a particular belief before doing anything and this is a good example of why. Someone else who felt suicidal might have felt no aversion to running that statement through the Belief Blaster but without asking there is no way of knowing. This response also made clear how serious the situation was.

I briefly described the nature of thoughts and beliefs, as I usually do when I first begin a session. I managed to get him to the point

For a personal consultation visit: www.themindhealer.co.uk

in which he at least accepted that in a sense, no belief is 100% accurate, and therefore we may as well identify beliefs which would more likely result in peace than stress and pain. It took a lot of trial and error but in the end he said ultimately he wanted to believe that "I will get better". However as soon as he said it he objected, saying that he had thought this many times but each time the bad feelings return.

In "PSTEC Advanced Part 2", I talked about the value in personifying certain thought processes in order to dissociate from them, therefore allowing a person to see the bigger picture. For example I have already described the Judge character who has lots of rules to be followed. In addition we also have a Villain who creates anger when the rules of the Judge aren't carried out and many more.

In this instance I decided to introduce the idea of characters to Mr G and said that there is a part of him which appears to be trying to protect him from becoming too hopeful about getting better. This part then dismisses any attempts to get better because it doesn't want any hopes to be built up, only to be shattered. He humoured me and came up with a silly name for the character at which point he again said that there is no point doing this as he has done something similar before. I immediately pointed out that there was his character in action, at which he laughed out loud.

Laughing at a problematic section of your model of reality is a huge step forward. I suggested that this part of him really did care and want the best for him but that it is actually doing the

For a personal consultation visit: www.themindhealer.co.uk

opposite. In fact it could be this character which was keeping him trapped feeling as he was. He agreed that this was possible.

With all of this in mind I told him to temporarily dismiss this part and for the moment say out loud "I will get better" over and over as if he really meant it. I advised him to imagine the days and weeks ahead getting so much better. He did so 7 times and I asked him to repeat. After the second round of saying it, his voice was beginning to sound much calmer and more confident. Next we progressed to "I will get better and stay better" which had a definite impact and he was feeling much calmer and seemed to be back to a safer frame of mind. He said that he had felt great for much of his life but just occasionally got into these bad frames of mind. He said he would call if he needed any further help.

I think this case really shows the raw power of this particular pre-talk about the nature of beliefs, in addition to finding just the right new idea to fire at their model of reality can have. On top of this, in a sense, we observed a problem "guard" at the castle and by becoming aware of it and characterising it, we were able to bypass it without difficulty. Bear in mind that no PSTEC tools were used in this severe situation, only some of the ideas on which they are based.

Panic Attacks

For a personal consultation visit: www.themindhealer.co.uk

Tim Phizackerley and Jeff Harding released an excellent audio product called the PSTEC Panic Attack sessions which has over 5 hours of material on how to use PSTEC to eradicate panic attacks. Rather than reinvent the wheel I thought it a good idea to present some of my thoughts on panic attacks as well as case studies which again show the framework already described in action.

The cause of panic attacks varies from person to person. For some a one off traumatic event may be the trigger whereas for someone else a build-up of events may be the cause. For yet others it could be a disempowering belief which is fuelling the fire and some actually have no idea consciously why the panic is surfacing. One thing they often have in common is that they find the panic attacks very unpleasant and often it feels as though they might be having a heart attack or losing their grip on reality.

This latter point often then creates a loop in which you fear the prospect of a panic attack, which in turn creates anxiety and thereby fuels an actual attack. A useful place to start whether you are a sufferer of panic attacks or a therapist is to reframe the panic to that of mere physical sensations. I ask in detail what they actually feel and they normally include things such as a racing heart, tightness in the chest and dizziness. I also find out how long they last and how frequently they occur. Although some people do have panic attacks which can take some time to dissipate, for most people it is all over within 5 minutes, though it might seem a lot longer whilst going through it.

I next liken it to a bad headache in a sense, in that it doesn't feel great but ultimately, like a headache it is merely an unwanted physical sensation in the body. I advise that if they feel one coming on, to take note of where they feel the sensations in their body and to take 5 slow deep breaths. After this they are again to note where the sensation is again in the body and whether it has increased/decreased/moved location, followed by another set of 5 slow deep breaths.

They are to repeat this process until they feel calm again. I suggest that whilst doing the above they are to think of themselves as a scientist whose job it is to monitor certain physical sensations. All of the above accomplishes 3 things:

1. It dissociates them to some extent from the panic by having them take the third party observer perspective.
2. Normally when a panic ensues, the sufferer will often have lots of disempowering thoughts about not being able to cope and wondering how long it will last, which in turn fuels the panic. Giving them a specific task like this to carry out interferes with their minds ability to throw fuel onto the fire.
3. The deep breathing physiologically counters the panic.

Hopefully the above reduces the risk of "fear of the fear" playing a role. By having a prearranged plan of action to carry out if one surfaces it can give them at least some sense of control in a situation which may otherwise feel completely out of their control.

For a personal consultation visit: www.themindhealer.co.uk

Once we have the above in place I will try to determine when the panic attacks started. I will also seek out any other painful events which may or may not on the surface seem related. In doing all of this I will also be on the lookout for potential beliefs that may have entered their model of reality just in case we need to work at the belief level. Here are a few case studies to illuminate this process in action.

Miss L - panic attacks

Miss L was a university student who was having multiple panic attacks daily. She had been quite a calm person until 2 years ago when the panic began. Although she hadn't made the link herself, her grandfather had died 2 years previously and it was few months after this the panic attacks began, seemingly out of the blue. The emotion linked to her grandfather's death was still very high and she wanted to see if we could take this lower.

Although the emotion was upset and sadness rather than anxiety, time and again I have cleared panic attacks for individuals, simply by clearing unresolved grief. One of our key universal human needs is a sense of certainty. When someone dies quickly and unexpectedly, not only do we feel a shock to the system and a great sense of loss, our sense of certainty also becomes disrupted. After all, when something or someone that seemed to be a permanent fixture in our lives suddenly goes, this has a knock on effect on our model of reality. It can leave us feeling in danger because the door becomes wide open as to what else might happen. This is especially the case if two or more very traumatic events occur in quick succession.

For a personal consultation visit: www.themindhealer.co.uk

In this instance Miss L responded well to the standard Click Tracks and felt more at peace when thinking about her grandfather. At this point in time she had zero anxiety about anything and wasn't able to bring bad feelings up even when trying. However, once we clear something big like this, it is impossible to say if further work is required until the dust has settled.

The week after Miss L returned to see me and her panic attacks began again two days later with no obvious trigger. At the beginning of any follow up session I always start by checking if our last work remains intact. She thought back to the painful memories of her grandfather and she still felt more at peace about that, which indicated that we had some more digging to do to see what else was playing a role.

Through conversation it appeared that the panic was associated with the pressure and stress she was feeling about her university work. She was able to feel an 8/10 anxiety at the thought of this. She focused on this and 3 Click Tracks later no change had occurred. We talked and it became evident that she didn't feel good enough.

She agreed that she was actually a high flying student and that the idea of "not being good enough" was neither useful nor true by any interpretation of it. We ran a PSTEC Negative on "I have the belief that I am not good enough" which surprisingly had little impact on her. Due to the complete lack of impact any of the tracks had had on her so far, I decided to try out a Cascade Release before getting onto inputting new beliefs.

As a quick reminder of what Cascade Release is, think of it as a Click Track which can be used directly on an emotion rather than on a known event. Throughout the track, the subconscious mind is instructed to identify every thought/belief/memory associated with the current feeling and is advised to fast forward it way into the distant future so that in a sense it hasn't happened yet. In phase two of the Cascade Release, the subconscious mind is instructed to remove all of the "badness" from the future and put it into the "trash can of the mind".

Although a Cascade Release isn't a track I would ever begin with under normal circumstances, it can produce some dramatic results where all else has failed. In this particular instance it did lower the anxiety a little, but more importantly a key piece of information was revealed to Miss L which proved vital in her recovery.

Miss L was very intelligent indeed but her older brother had done exceptionally well and a part of her didn't believe she could quite match his achievements in university and beyond. This then led to feelings of "not being good enough". We discussed potential new beliefs with which to frame this situation but a readymade one had come to her during the Cascade Release which was "I can achieve anything I set my mind on".

We tested this out by having her say it loud 7 times and then repeat this. Each time she verbalised the sentence the impact on

For a personal consultation visit: www.themindhealer.co.uk

her was visible and at the end we decided to stick with that sentence for the PSTEC Positive track. After the track she was literally buzzing.

Many months passed without any anxiety or panic whatsoever. She returned one day about 6 months later thinking that the anxiety had returned. The trigger appeared to be a fall out with a friend. As usual I checked in on our previous work with regard to achieving goals which had remained intact. I asked her to describe the feeling and her response was quite different to how she had described her anxiety previously. I asked if it might be anger that she was feeling given the circumstance and she realised it was. She agreed that the disagreement was over now and that the anger was no longer playing a useful role and it took just one Click Track to clear.

This case study shows the process in full swing once again. Removing the unresolved grief could quite easily have been enough to stop the panic but in her case the structure of the problem was a little more complex. At each step of the way we run a track or procedure, test and observe the response. Even if a particular step makes no measurable change in the symptoms, this lack of change is actually important information about where to go next.

At the point I used Cascade Release I could just as easily have used an Accelerator but the complete lack of change on the three previous Click Tracks that day, made me want to mix it up a little and use a slightly different method. Although the Cascade Release didn't budge the anxiety much, it prodded the model of

For a personal consultation visit: www.themindhealer.co.uk

reality to allow some useful information come to the surface which we were then able to use. After any track I check to see if the feelings have altered but also if any thoughts have sprung to mind throughout the process. Often nuggets like this can then be revealed.

Miss Y - Click Tracks mid panic attack

Miss Y had very dramatic panic attacks which left her incapacitated for hours after. Panic attacks of this length aren't common. When I first met her she had just started to have a panic attack in school and was shaking badly. The Click Tracks can seem a little odd to many people when they first come across them and require some concentration and focus, especially when you are just becoming familiar with the tapping process. Because of the required concentration, I suspect that anyone introduced to Click Tracks whilst in the middle of a panic attack might struggle to process the information and go along with the track. For this reason I allow them to simply copy me doing it.

Miss Y was sat opposite me shaking in her chair; her breathing was all over the place with tears in her eyes. She had never met me before so I kept my pretalk very brief. I gave her my name and told her to take slow deep breaths, which she tried but struggled to do. I told her that we were going to try a process which would hopefully help her out of the panic attack and that all she had to do was copy me. I told her that sometimes I would be tapping with one hand in times with some noises on the track, sometimes the other hand and at other times, both hands would be tapping together.

For a personal consultation visit: www.themindhealer.co.uk

I think to give her any more information in the state she was in would have been useless and she couldn't really speak to acknowledge that she'd heard me anyway. I pressed play on the standard Click Track and she followed along with my hand taps.

At the end she was still a little shaky but her breathing had returned to normal. I asked her a few questions such as if she had any favourite holiday destinations and after a few minutes she was able to go off back to class. The aim of that very brief session was purely to ease her out of the panic. What for her would normally last for hours lasted a mere 15 minutes. Another important and useful point to note is that if a person for whatever reason - whether they be very young, old or mid-panic - find it too much to follow the tapping instructions, it can work just as well by copying someone who is familiar with the process.

Suicidal

Miss S - suicidal thoughts and panic attacks

I have been describing some complex cases in which much more than the standard Click Tracks have been required. I have purposefully chosen such cases as it will illustrate information and potential ways forward when things don't quite go to plan. However, these are the outliers as many cases really are just straightforward. In other words in most situations there is a particular issue causing someone emotional distress; you have them think of the specifics, run a Click Track and the problem disappears never to return.

For a personal consultation visit: www.themindhealer.co.uk

The following case is a complex one which ran over multiple sessions but it also demonstrates what can be achieved with Click Tracks and working through the framework. Miss S had received help many times before seeing me to little avail. She had suicidal thoughts, intense self-hate, anger, ongoing panic attacks, anxiety and depression.

We identified the following sources of pain from her past.

- ❖ She was severely bullied for most of her school life.
- ❖ Her grandfather died 8 years ago and the pain is still very raw.
- ❖ She was very anxious about mother's ill health.
- ❖ Feelings of anger and rejection towards her absent father
- ❖ Major self-hate

Historical unresolved grief can be a huge contributing factor left intact. She had a 10/10 pain at the thought of her Nan. We ran through my grief pre-frame and she was happy to let it go if possible. One standard Click Track completely removed all grief and to her amazement she was unable to bring any back at that point in time. She actually thought initially that all the other pain had gone but when I had her think about the anger towards her father it quickly rose very high to a 9/10.

When we have a large number of events to plough through, if the first Click Track completely removes all of the pain from the focused on event, I always ask if the pain cleared quite quickly or

For a personal consultation visit: www.themindhealer.co.uk

it if went gradually over the course of the track. Miss J said that it disappeared very quickly. In order to do as much work as possible in the limited time I had with her, I experimented with the short Click Track 2015 (6 minutes long) on the anger towards father which disappeared after one listen.

Because there were a variety of emotions involved in the various things she had been through, rather than running a longer Click Track 2015 on one emotion I decided to pick each specific trauma off one at a time. I would alternate between the tapping Accelerator (due to its short length) and the short Click Track 2015. Each use of each track, I fast forwarded past the instructions straight to the tapping. Once they are familiar with the instructions I often do this when working in schools to a very tight time schedule in which I want to accomplish as much as possible in the limited time.

Within the space of 25 minutes we had removed very high emotions including unresolved grief, anxiety about mother, upset/anger about long term bullying as well as self-hate. For self-hate I simply have a person picture themselves in their mind's eye whilst trying to bring up the bad feeling and then run the track.

She felt like she was floating with all of this pain suddenly removed. We discussed various potential PSTEC Positive statements and she came up with "no more worries for the rest of your days". You wouldn't normally use the word "your" in a statement but this particular statement had particular relevance to her and when testing, greatly resonated so we stuck with it. She came into my office suicidal and left feeling like she didn't have a care in the world.

I suspected more work would be required once the dust had settled and indeed there was. Due to school holidays I was only able to see her a month later. She had been feeling great then a week after our session, some other pupils had been bullying her and she felt very anxious again.

I checked in on the work we did in our last session and all of it had remained intact other than the self-hate which had returned and anger, which was directed towards the bullies. Both feelings were a 10/10 and both cleared with one short Click Track 2015 each. Sometimes when a feeling comes back it can just mean that a little more Click Track work is required, but sometimes it can mean that some belief restructuring might need to be carried out. Even if I intend to carry out some restructuring, it is always best do it from a place of calm if possible, hence why I ran the Click Tracks first.

Digging deeper, it became clear that she hated herself because she thought she was ugly. I asked her when this belief was born and her first memory of it was when a boy broke up with her when she was 12 years old. As mentioned elsewhere I often use the idea of a belief being born in terms of the model of reality as it is a strange thing to say and helps dissociate them from their thoughts.

Together we analysed and deconstructed this idea; by this point we had great rapport and she was very on-board with the idea of a model of reality. Again, time was of the essence so rather than

For a personal consultation visit: www.themindhealer.co.uk

run a PSTEC Negative on the belief that she was ugly, I decided first to test new beliefs to see how well they stuck without first undoing the opposing belief. She came up with, "I need to keep my head up or my tiara will fall off" which for her really resonated just by saying it loud. We therefore went straight for the kill and ran this through PSTEC Positive which left her feeling giddy and happy. If nothing resonated I would have ran PSTEC Negative in an effort to undo the opposing belief first.

Many months had passed when she revisited me. She had been fine but something traumatic had occurred 4 weeks ago which she didn't want to divulge which led to her feeling completely overwhelmed. I asked if she was safe and if that she would feel safe if we took away some of the overwhelm. She agreed and also said that she had been severely self-harming ever since and showed me her arm which was cut to shreds. Apparently she had self-harmed for most of her life which had just stopped after the clearances we had made earlier in the year. She responded well as usual to the track but a week later she came back and said that the overwhelm had returned.

We cleared the overwhelm once more and this time she opened up to tell me what had happened. We discussed the trauma as well as her thinking around the topic. Between us we then brainstormed a number of different ways that we could perceive the event along with their corresponding emotional repercussions. We then settled on a way of thinking about it in which she felt that she was now safe and had learned from the experience. We also came up with specific behavioural strategies to reduce the risk of something similar occurring. We then

For a personal consultation visit: www.themindhealer.co.uk

constructed some PSTEC Positive statements to reflect the new viewpoint. In other words we got out a microscope, extracted the emotion from that specific point in her model of reality as before, but this time restructured the meaning as well to reduce the risk of a return of the pain.

Two weeks later the pain was gone from the event we worked on as well as everything else. This time though a little anxiety had arisen due to the thought that the bad feelings might all come back. I explained how our expectations can actually create problems out of thin air and she agreed we would better nipping this in the bud.

We proved this by having her say out loud a statement that she had come up with, "I can feel happy and free because everything is going to be ok". This felt good for her and so we ran a PSTEC Positive on it to ramp up the idea within her model of reality.

I saw her a few months later and her she was doing really well. Her self-esteem was high, she felt good about herself and all self-hate remained gone. She also told me that other than leaving her house for school, in the past she rarely left the house as she felt in danger. Our work had inadvertently cleared this too.

There are some key takeaways from this case study. When someone has been through so much, even when you clear all of the emotion, sometimes a little additional work needs to be done. Sometimes it is just a case of re-running a Click Track on a particular memory. Other times it is identifying problematic thoughts and choosing better ones to replace them with.

For a personal consultation visit: www.themindhealer.co.uk

Moreover, if she had been a private client, after the initial session she may have come to the conclusion that once the bad feelings returned that maybe PSTEC was just a temporary fix and therefore not booked in to see me again. The beauty of working in schools is that I often very quickly know if a problem has returned. I believe we did the bulk of the work in the first two sessions but the new ways of thinking hadn't quite solidified yet within her model of reality and therefore were susceptible to being nudged by other events occurring in life. By analysing what past work remains intact and what needs to be focused on in the moment we were able to fine tune the work required. For many people who have suffered a lot, quite often there is a need to prevent problems from being recreated due to bad expectations. In this case she could quite easily have led herself all the way back to self-hate and anxiety had we not nipped that bad "program" in the bud in the way that we did with PSTEC Positive.

Mr K - severe anxiety/multiple suicide attempts/inner voices/hallucinations

Mr K had made several serious suicide attempts over the past few years and felt like he couldn't continue. As have many people who see me, he had already been through the mill of psychiatrists, clinical psychologists, psychotherapists and counsellors but wasn't getting very far in terms of improving how he felt.

He had had a rough childhood and was still a teenager when he saw me. He didn't know his father and his mother had been a heroin addict who had died in prison a few years ago. He had been bullied in primary school at which point a fellow pupil had suggested he may as well jump off a bridge. He took this literally and was fortunately talked down off a motorway bridge by the police. The bully had apologised after this and the bullying stopped but he still felt very anxious and upset over this episode.

I suspect the background volatility in his life made him more susceptible to such a response to bullying. Only last week he had been back on top of the bridge but luckily came to his senses before he did anything. To begin we focused on the pain around the primary school bullying. Given his delicate emotional state I didn't have him bring up the bad feelings as much as possible but rather kept them as a 5/10 upset/anxiety. The first Click Track brought it down to a 3/10 and the second removed it completely. To his surprise he was unable to bring up any bad feelings about those memories once the track had finished.

Given the success of that I asked how he would feel about letting off some of the overwhelm he felt about his mother passing away. He was keen to let go of some of the 10/10 constant stomach churning he was feeling. One Click track brought it down a small amount but then we had a conversation in which he told me that he often hallucinates a person who follows him around everywhere. This person often tells him that he is worthless and that he should kill himself.

For a personal consultation visit: www.themindhealer.co.uk

The hallucination started off mostly at night but had started appearing during the day. He only realised it was a hallucination recently as people looked at him strangely when he was talking back to the person. Other mental health professionals were aware of this but seemed unable to help him. He said that the belief was "born" at the point he was being bullied in primary school.

He had already had my pre-talk on the nature of beliefs and he agreed that it would be useful to remove this particular belief. I initially view hallucinations/inner voices as a symptom of emotional pain rather than a problem in themselves. We ran a Belief Blaster on "I was worthless" which left him feeling very confused about the notion whereas beforehand it was just on obvious fact of reality to him that he was not worthy. He also yawned throughout the track which is always a good sign that releasing is taking place. He said that before the Belief Blaster he felt an intensity of 9/10 on the thought of suicide but after this it had come down to a 4/10 - the lowest it had been for a long time.

Next we discussed and tested potential new beliefs to replace the old one. As usual, once we came up with potentials I had him say them out loud 7 times to check how they felt. The one we settled on first was, "I can feel at peace because I am a good person". We had previously identified "peace" as a power word for him, as was the idea of being a good person.

We ran a PSTEC Positive on this after which he felt good. Just before this one of the potentials was a simple, "I am a good person" but it didn't quite feel right then. However after the previous track I had him test it again and this time it felt right.

For a personal consultation visit: www.themindhealer.co.uk

This is always something to be aware of; each time a piece of work is done, the model of reality changes and therefore something that might have been rejected beforehand might now be accepted. Following this he felt zero suicidal impulses and felt calmer than he remembered feeling for years.

I saw him again a week later. He had felt great for two days following our session, during which time the thought of being worthless was far from his mind. However on the third day the feelings returned with a bang. Why was this? It is impossible to say with certainty but I suspect a few factors may have played a role. First of all, he had thought a particular way for so long that the old "pathways" and ways of thinking had been changed but weren't far enough past the tipping point on the scales of belief change to stick. Secondly I had recommended his carer purchase PSTEC Positive so that he could feed the new ways of thinking to increase the chance of locking them in place but this hadn't happened.

This time we tried PSTEC Negative on "I have the belief that I am worthless" which he said produced a noticeable shift. However when we tested the previous PSTEC Positive statements, they no longer resonated. After playing around with different ideas we came up with a statement which acknowledged his imperfections whilst at the same time indicating that he was going to be ok.
"I might not be perfect but I am going to be ok"

This had a definite positive impact so we ran it seven times to put as much weight onto that side of the belief scale as possible.

In a statement like this you would normally avoid using words like "not". For example the words "I might be imperfect" would be better. However the statement as written resonated more for him so I decided to go with that. Finally we ended with a few "everything is going to be ok" PSTEC Positives. This barrage of PSTEC Positives brought his anxiety down from high to a 1/10, which again was one of the lowest levels it had been for a long time. Each time we ran the PSTEC Positive track the bad feeling came down one point and so I think this shows that sometimes you really need to pile on those empowering suggestions.

The following time I saw him, there was still some background anxiety but he felt more neutral about himself. We discussed potential activities that he could do to create more fun and variety into his life. He mentioned that he used to go to a boxing gym and that this definitely impacts his anxiety but he hadn't been for a while. We then went on to create an exercise schedule for him, which included running, boxing and other sports. He saw me a week later feeling great and we didn't have to do any work on that occasion. Sadly, after this, he was due to leave that school for another. I would have preferred for him to have several weeks of feeling ok but so long as he carried out the PSTEC Positive homework he had a good chance of staying mentally healthy.

As you can see in this case study, it's almost like a dance with the person's model of reality. Some things stick, others don't. Sometimes all is good but a life event occurs which knocks a useful belief over, indicating that its roots weren't quite deep enough to stay intact. Also this case shows that sometimes multiple PSTEC Positives might be the best way to go. I also strongly suspect that adding exercise and activity into his life will increase the chance of maintaining his feelings of calm and self-worth, which in turn seemed to be keeping hallucinations from appearing.

Inner Voices

Mr G - Anxiety and inner voices

Above I described quite a complex case which involved hallucinations. I have helped many people with visual hallucinations as well as those who hear inner voices. I initially see them primarily as a symptom of distress and therefore treat them like I would any other person suffering from anxiety.

Mr G had been hearing the voice of a man since the age of 5 years old. Most of what the man said was of no consequence but sometimes it got very angry. Sometimes it would call him things such as "stupid" or "idiot". He had recently begun feeling very distressed because he had had an argument with his mother and the voice told him to kill her. The distress was down to it being an upsetting thing to hear, not any fear that he might end up hurting his mother.

People who hear "voices" are often very anxious about this fact. Anxiety itself can bring about such symptoms and therefore I aim to make them feel a bit more at ease with the idea of hearing inner voices. I explain that anxiety and stress can produce all sorts of seemingly strange symptoms, one of them being an inner

For a personal consultation visit: www.themindhealer.co.uk

voice that feels as though it isn't coming from within. I go on to suggest that once we clear as much anxiety and stress from a person's life, most of the time the voice just disappears or at least doesn't bother them in any way.

I then proceeded as I would with any case of anxiety, first by identifying when it began and also noting any significant events which are still emotionally charged. There were two cases of unresolved grief involving a pet and a grandparent (unresolved grief for a pet can be every bit as distressing as that for a human) which were both emotionally charged.

Also quite tellingly, his parents separated when he was 5 years old, at which point the inner voice began. He had no emotion linked to this event. I asked if he saw his father and did he get on with him. He did get on with him but when I asked he said he does feel a bit anxious when with father but doesn't know why. I asked if the voice in his head sounded anything like his father and he seemed shocked to realise that it sounded very like him.

We quickly cleared the unresolved grief as well as the unexplained anxiety at the thought of his father without any difficulty with a Click Track. I asked if he was able to bring up any anxiety at the thought of the voice now and he couldn't. He was able to before and the reason I hadn't run a Click Track directly on that, is because by clearing the other emotions first, whether anxiety about the voice remained would give a clue as to its cause. If it had remained I would have simply ran a Click Track on that. We ended with a PSTEC Positive on, "no matter what happens, everything is going to be ok".

For a personal consultation visit: www.themindhealer.co.uk

I saw him a month later and again much later but the voice never returned and he remained anxiety free.

Mr L - psychic inner voices

I include this case study because it was quite intriguing. Mr L was feeling very anxious because an inner voice had sprung up out of nowhere in the past few months and began making predictions which all appeared to be coming true. When asked for examples, he told me that he often gets a thought that someone is looking at him from behind and when he turns around there is actually someone there doing just that.

Just before being given homework, the voice might tell him exactly what the homework will be and will always be right etc. More sinisterly, the voice had predicted that a man in a white van would pull up to him on his way home from school and ask for directions and that there would be a terrorist attack at a particular airport in Europe at the weekend (the voice gave specifics).

There appeared to be no turmoil other than a little more stress than usual in school due to increased workload. I thought it best to think of a way of framing the situation which would help alleviate some of his stress. I knew some of his interests and that he was into comic superheroes so I suggested that rather than being stressed at these strange symptoms, why not think of it as a superpower? He liked the idea of this and had a big grin on his face.

For a personal consultation visit: www.themindhealer.co.uk

Although I am not a believer in psychic powers, that weekend I certainly paid a little more attention to the news than normal but thankfully the predicted terrorist attack didn't occur. However, when I next saw him he told me that a man in a van had pulled up to ask for directions as predicted. He seemed more relaxed about it all and I took this particular prediction with a pinch of salt.

Fast forward 3 weeks and everything became clear. His parents were separating and he was feeling very stressed about this fact. I suspect he was initially telling the truth about the coincidences which had been occurring but with the bigger and more definite predictions had been more of a cry for help. I also believe that he was only semi-aware that his parents might be separating and therefore may not have been consciously aware of why he was so anxious. We ran some Click Tracks and belief restructuring which left him feeling calmer about his parents and the psychic inner voice disappeared for good.

Miss Q - plotting to kill everyone

Here is one last case study in this genre of anxiety and stress causing unusual symptoms. Miss Q was very distressed about certain thoughts she was having and it took some rapport building before she felt comfortable enough to tell me. Her mind constantly came up with methods of how to kill whoever she was with. She had no desire or intention to kill anyone and therefore found the thoughts very upsetting. I asked if she had figured out

For a personal consultation visit: www.themindhealer.co.uk

how she would kill me to which she replied: Yes. I didn't ask how.

Instead I ignored this symptom and identified current and historical pain points in her life. The key one was being bullied 10 years previously when she was a teenager, which was still very emotionally charged when thinking about it. We ran one Click Track to clear all the anger, anxiety and upset from these memories. She contacted me 3 weeks later saying that the visions of violence had stopped since the session. It is impossible to say for sure but maybe when she was being bullied, as a way to feel more powerful maybe she imagined hurting the bullies. If a specific thought is repeated in a state of high emotional arousal it can easily become locked in place and continue for years left unchecked, even if the trigger events stopped long ago.

Health Scares

This is a key area which can easily be overlooked by therapists and self-helpers, especially if the health scare has passed and all is ok. For example, I helped a man who had been suffering from gradually worsening panic attacks for the past 12 months. He couldn't think of any triggers but one of the key questions I ask is whether they or anyone close to them had any health scares at any point. He acknowledged that his brother had been seriously ill last year but that he was fine now.

I had him focus on this event and to his surprise his anxiety went through the roof. He couldn't understand why this was the case given that all was ok now with his brother. I reminded him that it doesn't make the slightest bit of difference whether something seems big on paper; the important thing to note is whether an event or memory brings up any emotion. If it does, this suggests that within their model of reality, the subconscious mind still attributes a lot of emotional significance to the event.

We cleared the emotion with a Click Track and followed up with some PSTEC Positives around the idea that everything was going to be ok and this stopped his panic attacks on the spot. A few months later he contacted me to say that all of his anxiety had dissipated and he was doing great.

Generalised Anxiety

There is a condition called Generalised Anxiety Disorder by psychologists. In these scenarios there doesn't appear to be an obvious trigger but I have found that in many cases there is a cause; it is just that it is not known to the person suffering. Talking therapies often take some time to make an impact in these instances.

Again whatever symptoms or labels are presented to me by a client, I go through the process and framework in the same way. Often there is a historical cause that perhaps the client had dismissed or is unaware of.

A key question I always ask people, who have been diagnosed with this (or are otherwise suffering from anxiety with no

For a personal consultation visit: www.themindhealer.co.uk

obvious cause) is if they feel that danger is just around the corner. Many say that indeed it does feel as though danger is imminent but they cannot say why or where this danger is coming from.

Having already explained the nature of thoughts, beliefs and the model of reality, I suggest that the belief that they are in danger is actually trying to serve a useful purpose in trying to protect them. By generating the anxiety that part of them feels as though they are a little safer. However, I explain that when we are in a state of constant anxiety, in some ways it is more difficult to respond to any potential danger or stressors because we are worn out and overwhelmed.

I then suggest that in fact, from a place of calm we would actually be safer as well as enjoy life much more. Most people follow this train of thinking intellectually but don't feel it. This in essence, is one area in which cognitive and talking approaches can benefit from the approaches described in this book with tools such as PSTEC.

An option here is to run a PSTEC Negative on, "I have the belief that danger is just around the corner" or whatever variance of that which resonates the most. I then follow it up with a PSTEC Positive statement along the lines of "Everything is going to be ok", the wording dependent on the specific client and what feels best for them. This combination is extremely effective for anxiety sufferers, especially once historical pain has been removed with the Click Tracks.

For a personal consultation visit: www.themindhealer.co.uk

Mr A - Generalised anxiety

Mr A was a successful businessman, appeared confident, was happily married and on the surface didn't seem to have anything to be concerned about. However he had recently been diagnosed with Generalised Anxiety Disorder. The anxiety was high and constant in the background no matter what he was doing. Medication and Cognitive Behaviour Therapy had had little effect over the years so he decided to try something different.

We identified a few key events which had some emotional charge but there was nothing that massively stood out. As we went further back on his timeline into the 0-10 year old range, he changed the topic and said that despite being surrounded by friends and family who he was very close to, he just felt alone and didn't know why. This thought seemed to bring up his anxiety so I kept a mental note of this for once we had completed the time line procedure, to check for any relevant early childhood events.

He was just about to say that there was nothing of note during that time period when his eyes opened wide and a key memory revealed itself. He was about 5 years old and was out shopping with his mother. He was hiding from her behind some clothes on a rack and then she had gone. Looking back as an adult, he figured that his mother probably panicked when she couldn't see him and ran outside to see if she could see him out there.
Of particular interest here is that the feelings of being all alone came right up to a 10/10 and he was visibly shaken. What was probably only about 30 second later his mother came back into

For a personal consultation visit: www.themindhealer.co.uk

the shop to pick up her sobbing child. However for a small child who thinks they have lost a parent, 30 seconds can seem like an eternity. We ran a Click Track on this event which cleared after one listen despite being very high. This is common with historical events when the adult looking back can see with clarity an alternative and calmer viewpoint/reality tunnel.

After this he felt very calm and confused. The feelings of being alone had gone for the moment but I wanted to hedge our bets and came up with some PSTEC Positive statements to ram home the fact that he is surrounded by people who love him. Doing so gave him a very warm and tingly feeling around his body. For him this was the end of his Generalised Anxiety Disorder.

As with panic attacks, it isn't always a one session fix and sometimes additional and ongoing work is required. Once obvious potential past and present causes have been eliminated with the Click Tracks, if the anxiety remains, I would experiment with the Accelerator track to see if we can seek out any hidden historical cause.

I would also consider using the Cascade Release track which can produce amazing results when an emotion is felt but the cause isn't known. I would have the person say out loud, "it is safe to feel safe" and "I am safe" to check for any subconscious resistance in the form of unpleasant emotions. Remember that if you say something that your subconscious mind disagrees with, the incongruence will be felt within, which is why this is such a powerful method for uncovering hidden beliefs.

If resistance does surface to those statements, I would go through different potential beliefs with the client that they may be holding to see which one "fits". Often, as I mentioned earlier in this section, there is a belief about being in imminent danger, or about being in danger if they feel calm. I have worked with so many people for whom these beliefs are a self-evident aspect of reality and they initially look at me in shock when I suggest that we get rid of them.

However once I explain the reasoning as discussed earlier and they consider that they might actually be safer in a place of calm, I haven't yet had a person who doesn't then want to remove the belief with PSTEC Negative. We often follow up with potential statements such as, "from now on I can feel calm and safe". Of course the specifics would depend on what resonates with the client.

As I mentioned earlier in the book, one of our key human needs is a sense of certainty. When this sense of certainty is put into doubt, anxiety is often the result. When constructing PSTEC Positive statements, especially for those suffering from anxiety, one of my aims is to fulfil this sense of certainty through the ideas we come up with.

"Certainty" after all is just a concept within the model of reality. Ultimately none of us can be certain of anything. However focusing on the concept from this perspective serves no useful purpose. I often give the example of when people are driving on the road and very often there are cars coming in the opposite direction very quickly just a meter or two away (I do not use this

For a personal consultation visit: www.themindhealer.co.uk

example if the person has a fear of cars or driving). Most of us don't dwell on this thought as we are normally just focused on getting to where we are headed. In a sense, we just have to have faith that everything will be ok.

Another way of saying this is that it makes sense to take any obvious precautions but after that to assume everything will be ok. This is why the statement, "no matter what happens, everything will be ok" is so powerful. Especially when prefaced with the idea that of course life comes with its ups and down but we can develop a sense of certainty that we will be able to deal with whatever crops up.

Obtaining Information from Your Anxiety

Contained within anxiety is often useful information and sometimes it can alert you to potential dangers which might not be obvious on the surface. I am bit of a risk taker and a quite a few years ago I left a safe, well paid job in IT in the middle of the biggest recession in decades. I was leaving it to pursue my hobbies of hypnotherapy, Spanish guitarist and psychological magic with a strong focus on the entertainment.

Many of my friends and family were scratching their heads wondering what was going through my mind. Although I had already had many clients by this time, I certainly didn't have an ongoing client base. In fact I had zero clients booked moving forward on the day I left the job. Moreover, with the music and magic, I did have a few gigs each week but in any recession, non-

For a personal consultation visit: www.themindhealer.co.uk

essentials like entertainment can be the first thing to go. Even when the economy is going well work can dry up without warning.

I had big bills to pay each month and zero certainty that I would be able to pay them. However for me it was a no brainer because I hated the thought of working in IT for the rest of my life and I was utterly determined to make a success of my new ventures. This single mindedness didn't remove all of my anxiety which stood at around the 8/10 mark (although this was part excitement too probably; the physiological differences between the two are negligible). It was obvious to me that a part of me was worried about the bills and the potential for failure.

I brainstormed some backup plans to see if I could settle that part of me. In fact I came up with several options just in case the worst came to the worst. This act in itself brought down the anxiety to a 4/10 but I focused some more to see if there was any other useful information to be gained but I couldn't come up with anything more. I therefore concluded that the background 4/10 anxiety wasn't serving any useful purpose and was merely using up energy which I could be using to make a success of things. I therefore ran one Click Track which cleared the emotion away and ran a PSTEC Positive on the statement "No matter what happens, everything will be OK". This felt better for me than a direct, "I am going to make a success of this!" type statement and I suspect this was the case because it acknowledged the possibility of ups and downs whilst still allowing me to envision success.

For a personal consultation visit: www.themindhealer.co.uk

This subtle technique of listening in to the emotion can be very revealing, especially when much of a person's historical trauma have been cleared. Simply focus on the feeling and just ask "why?" or "what is this about" a few times and see what crops up. If something does reveal itself you can work directly on that. Otherwise you are free to play around with the Accelerators, Cascade Release or the standard emotion clearing Click Tracks. When using the latter but you aren't sure what to think about, just choose something that it could be, or even visualise what the anxiety would look like if it was in front of you. This is just to give the mind something to aim at.

This is especially good for little niggles that you can't quite figure out what the cause is. When you do come up with a potential cause, observe how you are thinking about the situation and try to come up with several other ways of thinking about the same situation to see if any of the alternatives feel better. If they do, construct potential PSTEC Positive statements to reflect the new way of thinking and begin saying them out loud for testing. Once you have found the best one, run it through PSTEC Positive and in many cases you will be pleasantly surprised when the niggle just disappears. Doing this is literally like micromanaging your model of reality when it isn't working as you'd like it to.

Psychosis

Miss Z

Miss Z had suffered terribly throughout most of her childhood and both arms were completely cut to pieces through self-harm. She had been diagnosed with psychosis and felt she had a demon in her head which spoke to her and terrified her. In fact, whilst I was speaking to her, she would occasionally have a look of horror on her face and when I asked what had just happened she told me the demon had just said something. I had been asked to see her because she had an intense fear of needles and had a doctor's appointment the following week which was terrifying her.

Following my usual pre-talk I asked if she would like to see if we could turn down some of the anxiety she had about needles. When it comes to removing phobias such as this I always tell the client that they still might not like needles once the fear has been cleared but that they should feel calmer about it. In the past I have had people think they still had a phobia despite all the fear disappearing because in their head, they seem to think that they should now quite like the object of fear. Most people who have their fear of spiders removed still don't particularly like them but if they had to, they could pick one up. By guiding a person's definition of success/failure, the risk of them incorrectly thinking they still have the phobia reduces.

One standard Click Track removed her fear of needles and she was unable to bring back the fear. She was very intrigued by the speed with which the process worked. She was terrified of the demon inhabiting her head and a quick scan through her life showed up no obvious traumas. I often have clients think about different people in their life to see if any bad feelings come up

For a personal consultation visit: www.themindhealer.co.uk

and major anxiety came up when thinking about her father, though she had no idea why. She agreed that it might help her if we removed this anxiety and so we ran a Click Track. Near the end the "demon" said something which interfered with the process but this was right near the end of the track and she still had very high anxiety when thinking about her father.

She saw her father regularly and enjoyed his company and said that despite the anxiety, she felt safe with him. An Accelerator track brought no causal events to mind and she said that she would be happy and feel safe if the anxiety was removed. Just in case there was a genuine subconscious reason for the anxiety we chatted and it was clear that there was definitely no immediate danger to her in removing the fear and maybe this was a by-product of some historical misunderstanding or even her psychosis. We identified the belief she had as, "I have the belief that my father is dangerous". She laughed at this thought but said it felt very real at the same time. After running PSTEC Negative through this she had zero anxiety about her father. Sadly this was at a school I only visit very occasionally and so wasn't able to follow this up.

There is a school of thought amongst certain psychologists that the cause of certain "disorders" such as psychosis and schizophrenia are largely a product of emotional distress. Although there may well be a genetic/brain chemistry factor involved sometimes, the people I have worked with so far exhibiting these kinds of symptoms, have had a full or partial removal of the hallucinations/inner voices once their emotional distress has been alleviated. It will be interesting to see how tools

For a personal consultation visit: www.themindhealer.co.uk

like PSTEC change the perception of treating problems such as this as it becomes more well established.

If I were given the chance to work further with Miss Z I would attempted to restructure her fear around the "demon" via Click Tracks, belief restructure and reframing. In my view I am working with the content of her model of reality and so long as the "demon" has emotional significance it will continue to form part of her day to day life.

Phobias

Many phobias are straightforward in that a person feels excessive and irrational fear about something and they would rather not. Simple phobias often require a Click Track when thinking about the problem in question and in most cases the fear should evaporate quite quickly. Contrast this with complex phobias which have a deeper underlying structure and often, the surface level anxiety is a way to protect the person from another perceived danger. I talked about this in PSTEC in the Trenches but think it will be useful to give a few more examples here within the framework set out.

Mr W - fear of flying

Tim Phizackerley and I have a business called Fly and Be Calm. Tim used his genius to create an audio package for fearful flyers which includes emotion clearing tracks as well as more hypnotic style tracks specific to the fear of flying. We have partnered with many big players in the UK aviation industry and for the vast majority of self-helpers the tracks just work. If you would like to check out further information on this and see videos of it in action, please visit http://www.flyandbecalm.co.uk.

Nothing like this can be 100% successful however and it is in the outliers that we can demonstrate different ways of working when things don't quite go to plan. Mr W had used the Fly and Be Calm system but it wasn't having the usual dramatic impact. His flight was coming up and he requested a personal session with me.

I hunted around his past but found nothing of note, which suggests that a complex phobia may be in play. He knew intellectually that flying was the safest form of transport as most people do, but it didn't help. We ran the Accelerators, Cascade Release and a PSTEC Negative on the idea of flying being dangerous. He had already listened to the Fly and Be Calm tracks extensively so we tried the Click Track 2015 which contains different suggestions to no avail.

It is only in more recent years that I have really understood the power and importance of PSTEC Positive and spending time coming up with the perfect statement and combination of ideas for that particular person at that time. In fact, although I will rarely begin a session with PSTEC Positive, when nothing else works this is where I spend nearly all of my time with a client. We discussed various options and he finally settled on the very powerful, "I've got this!". We had played around with various

For a personal consultation visit: www.themindhealer.co.uk

other concepts and ideas and tested them by saying them out loud but this one in particular had a definite impact on his physiology.

We ran it through PSTEC Positive a few times whilst picturing him being calm on his upcoming flight. The result was a complete cessation of all of his anxiety. He utilised the track on that statement leading up to his flight and was calm throughout.

There are various reasons why statements such as these can be so powerful for people. First of all it isn't making any promises that everything will be ok. Rather it creates a sense of **certainty** that the person will be able to deal with a particular situation. By making it non-specific as well as emotive (in a positive sense), these kinds of statements are often met with less resistance and the emotion that comes with them helps to lock them in place. This doesn't mean that you should always have a non-specific statement. Only through testing will it become apparent what the person's model of reality needs at that particular time.

Miss C - complex fear of flying

Miss C had flown around the world for most of her life without a problem. In the past few years her anxiety had begun to grow and now, in her job, she had to travel all over Europe via car. She attended numerous "fear of flying" courses as well as visiting numerous therapists to no avail. She was able to bring up anxiety at the thought of flying but the various Click Tracks weren't budging it.

For a personal consultation visit: www.themindhealer.co.uk

We discussed various life events which had occurred, some of which were traumatic. When identifying historical traumas, if a particular scenario seems unrelated to the current issue I try to determine if the concepts involved could be interpreted as a similar pattern by the model of reality when compared with the presenting issue.

When Miss C was 7 years old her father was lost at sea. There was background sadness at this memory but nothing major as it was many years ago. However, she admitted that it was a very difficult time for her as she didn't really have one primary caregiver and was passed from pillar to post. Drilling further, I uncovered two facts which seemed relevant. Firstly, her own daughter was approaching the age of 7 years old when Miss C's fear began. Secondly, at around this time she had been on a flight on which the turbulence was bad which shook her up.

As I have mentioned before I often try to form theories about what is happening, even if they can't always be proven/disproven. I suggested that maybe the bad flight occurring at the same time that her daughter was approaching the same age that Miss C had been when her father became lost at sea, may have been playing a role. She stared ahead and said that makes perfect sense. A lot of upset came up shortly after, as she said that it was the thought of something happening to her and then her daughter being passed around as she had been as a child which seemed to be causing the upset (Miss C's partner wasn't on the scene).

For a personal consultation visit: www.themindhealer.co.uk

An emotional response to a particular theory is indicative that there is some truth in it. We ran a track on the upset that came up which disappeared after one listen. Now the thought was out in broad daylight, she realised that in the unlikely event that anything did happen to her, they were very close to her brother's family and that they would likely take her daughter under their wing.

Next we came up with some PSTEC Positive statements to reinforce the idea that both she and her daughter were both going to be ok. She felt very at peace and was unable to bring up any anxiety at the thought of flying or anything else. Sadly, I lost her contact details and wasn't able to see how she got on with her flight but I am quietly confident that she would have been ok.

This case really did have a complicated origin, whereas the previous case was complex only in that what he needed more than anything else was confirmation that he would be able to handle the flight no matter what.

Mr S – Emetophobia (fear of being sick)

The fear of being sick is quite common. In one of the first schools I worked at, a boy was barely able to leave his house due to this fear. Two months previously he had felt sick in class and had to rush to the toilets. He wasn't actually sick in the end and he went back to class and all was ok. However, this thought of being sick in front of a group of people played on his mind and the more he thought about it, the more it dominated his mind.

For a personal consultation visit: www.themindhealer.co.uk

A few weeks on he couldn't even face going to school and moving on from there the thought of leaving the house was becoming distressing for him, just in case he was sick in front of anyone. Sometimes phobias and anxiety can become worse over time if left untreated and the fear itself can become something to be feared. Mr S was aware of my work in schools and although he had had counselling he knew that my techniques might be worth a try given how different they were.

He braved coming into school specifically to see me and I presented the idea of a model of reality and the nature of beliefs etc. We got to a point in which he agreed that the chances of him actually being sick in front of someone were actually very slim (in the past 15 years he had never done so). Also, he agreed that the thought of being sick in front others is unpleasant for anyone but that the excessive anxiety and embarrassment his model of reality were creating for him weren't doing him any good at all.

This initial conversation was aimed at bypassing as much potential resistance to just clearing the anxiety and embarrassment as possible prior to running the Click Track. I had him relive the memory in which he was nearly sick but this time to imagine he actually was sick in class. This brought up 9/10 embarrassment and anxiety. A Click Track and an EEF cleared this and his emetophobia and fast developing agoraphobia (fear of open spaces/leaving the house) disappeared completely. We didn't have time for any PSTEC Positives but ultimately they weren't needed.

Miss P - complex emetophobia

Miss P was a schoolgirl who had recently turned into a school refuser, apparently due to a severe fear of vomiting. Severe anxiety was also produced when hearing and seeing someone else vomit. This was rapidly beginning to impact her life more and more as time went on. Rather than assume a complex phobia, it always makes sense to treat it as a simple phobia and progress depending on what happens.

First she thought back to a time when she was actually very sick a few years ago. Oddly, at the time, she dealt with it well but afterwards when thinking about it, the anxiety ramped up. The anxiety came up high just thinking about it but one Click Track cleared it right down. Next we used YouTube to search for videos of people being sick as she was now unable to bring up the fear using imagination alone.

Videos did indeed bring up the anxiety and she ran a Click Track whilst watching the video. Her father was amazed as this appeared to be a huge breakthrough for her and something that would have made her very upset and anxious prior to our work. We ended with some PSTEC Positive statements through experimentation which acknowledged that being sick isn't nice but that she was safe.

She admitted that she felt very calm and her anxiety about vomiting did indeed seem to have gone. I left and spoke to her father a few days later who said that as soon as I left she began crying, saying that no change had occurred. This didn't make

For a personal consultation visit: www.themindhealer.co.uk

much sense as her father could see the huge change in her following the Click Tracks and the fact that she was able to watch the YouTube videos from a place of calm suggested that something was amiss.

Through conversation, I found out that at around the time she was sick, her grandparent and a family pet had died. Having come across many such similar situations, I theorised that maybe Miss P felt that she might not see her parents again if she left them. This was congruent with the nature of her grandparent and pet passing away, in that she wasn't able to see either due to sickness. I was then told that even if she is in the house she does get very fretful if not with both parents. I suggested having her run through the Click Track on those painful events.

For various reasons I wasn't able to get an update over the summer holidays. However, I heard through the school that she was back in school and happy to be there. I don't believe Miss P was consciously aware of all that was going on within her mind and I also believe that there was definitely some anxiety over the idea of vomiting. However this is another case in which identifying and working with the hidden underlying structure is what produced the result.

Miss J - fear of needles with no desire to change

This is a scenario which won't crop up for most people. Either they will be a self-helper who actually wants to remove a phobia or a therapist for whom paying clients want help to remove a phobia. Fear of needles is one in which people can sometimes

For a personal consultation visit: www.themindhealer.co.uk

put their own life in danger by avoiding a blood test or some of other critical course of action involving needles.

I have had half a dozen people in recent times who had meningitis in very early childhood which resulted in lots of needles and a long stay in hospital. It is understandable that going through an experience such as that so early in life could cause the brain to try to avoid that kind of scenario in future.

Whatever the cause, we have a problem if someone is so deeply embedded within their phobic reality tunnel that they put themselves in danger. So if someone is dead against help but badly needs it, how can they be helped?

I have found a subtle frame through which I can often bypass resistance in cases such as these. Miss J is one of those people who had some very bad early experiences in hospitals with needles. There was major resistance to letting go of the fear on top of the belief that the Click Tracks would never work on this anyway. I had already guided Miss J through clearing some major trauma; each time she would emphatically claim that nothing could ever clear this pain, yet each time one or two rounds of Click Tracks did just that.

We had great rapport and I suggested that if we just cleared anxiety at the thought of needles, then she can still choose not to have any injections but that she would be carrying less bad feelings in her system. This made sense to her and didn't alarm her guards who were there to keep her from needles.

For a personal consultation visit: www.themindhealer.co.uk

After the Click Track she went from a 10/10 upset and anxiety to calm. Even then she was still determined that it would be different if an actual needle was used. The next time we managed to get hold of a needle and again used the idea that the intention wasn't for her to have any needle work done, just to let go of some bad feelings overall.

We proceeded in this manner and with much of the bad feeling gone, the reality tunnel she had been trapped in was now much weaker and through the way she spoke it was already clear that she was more open to the idea of having a blood test.

At the time of writing this is an ongoing case but I am very confident that she could now manage to have a blood test or injection when her next trip to the hospital is due. This might seem deceptive on the surface but no-one is being forced to do anything. Rather we are using the Click Track to at least give her a real choice whereas with the panic intact, the decision had already been made for her via a conclusion her 3 year old brain had arrived at.

Obsessive Compulsive Disorder (OCD)

This is a common complaint and is often combined with a lot of anxiety and obsessive thinking and behaviour. Traditional therapy sometimes struggles to make headway on this "disorder" without a lot of ongoing work. Regardless of labels, I simply identify what behaviours, thoughts and emotions are causing

For a personal consultation visit: www.themindhealer.co.uk

distress and then run through the framework I set out at the beginning of the book. Once historical pain is removed we then set to work on removing emotions linked to the OCD behaviours and restructuring thoughts if required.

Mr L - obsessive hand washing

For the past 2 years Mr L had washed his hands continuously throughout the day and as a result they were red raw. He had a strong desire to stop but felt unable to. We went through his personal history but other than little niggles here and there, nothing of note sprang out. I asked if he could bring up anxiety or any other emotion at the thought of not washing his hands but he couldn't do it on demand.

Using a process I first described in "PSTEC in the Trenches" I had him say out loud something which I knew would cause him distress if he actually meant it, "I am never washing my hands ever again" and this immediately brought up an 8/10 anxiety. I cannot emphasise enough how powerful these techniques are which involve saying out loud certain statements, either to prod the model of reality to bring up some of the bad feelings, or to test if certain beliefs are held there subconsciously.

We ran a standard Click Track on the idea of never washing his hands again and the anxiety disappeared. He was unable to bring it back on demand and when saying the statement out loud again, nothing came up which was a good sign and a good way to test our work. Next we came up with a strategy for moving forward. We couldn't assume at this point that the compulsion would

For a personal consultation visit: www.themindhealer.co.uk

remain completely gone and there was also an element of habit involved.

We therefore planned in advance when a typical person might wash their hands and he agreed that that would be a good thing to aim for. Next, I framed a compulsion as a mere emotion, or physical sensation which is trying to guide him to take a particular action. I suggested that if any such compulsion came along, that he should observe where he feels the compulsion in his body and run it through the Click Track. I saw him a month later, his hands looked fine and he said that he hadn't needed to do any further work after our session.

Mr C - OCD, tics and gambling addiction

A few months previously Mr C's father had passed away and as a result he was struggling with work and day to day life. He could feel a deep churning in the pit of his stomach constantly and was struggling to cope. The first time I saw him he had exhibited none of the symptoms which developed later.

Because he was struggling so much he wanted to see if we could turn down some of the overwhelm he was experiencing. A few Click Tracks later and the stomach churning had gone. This was a very good result considering it was an immediate family member and so recent. I expected to have to do a little more work and maybe create some PSTEC Positive statements moving forward.

For a personal consultation visit: www.themindhealer.co.uk

I saw him a few weeks later and he was still doing much better but his stomach churning had returned but was much lower than it had been previously. This was cleared with another Click Track. He did fine for the following 6 months but when I next saw him he had developed quite severe tics and by all accounts had a gambling addiction and was exhibiting OCD type symptoms. His OCD mostly came in the form of assuming disaster will strike if he doesn't reach a certain place on the pavement by the time a random car got there.

The gambling mostly came in the form of internet gambling and he carried a small pack of cards around with him, yet when he looked at them he seemed anxious. It is impossible to say if the OCD, Tics and gambling came directly as an after effect of the grief he felt for his father. He said there was still stomach churning there but that the work we had done had largely remained intact on that front and it was minimal by comparison.

It seemed that many of the symptoms of his current problems were anxiety related. I theorised that perhaps the sudden death of his father had put a huge dent in his certainty in the world and that as a result, his anxiety was pouring out in various ways.
He was feeling overwhelmed and his tics were quite severe so to begin with we ran a Click Track 2015 medium length (about 12 minutes) twice whilst he thought about everything that had happened. At the end he felt considerably calmer and his tics had diminished substantially. Next we broke down the structure of his current behaviours and came up with strategies to overcome the OCD and gambling addiction.

For a personal consultation visit: www.themindhealer.co.uk

As in most cases I explained how we all consist of different parts and that a part of him really did believe that if he didn't reach the traffic light or street lamp before a car got there, then he would be in grave danger. I also asked if there is a part of him which knows that this isn't true, despite feeling very true and he agreed that there was.

I then went on to explain that this part of him is just trying to protect him but that it is just a little misguided. It was influencing his thoughts and behaviour through anxiety. Therefore if we turned down the emotional power backing these OCD type thoughts and scenarios, then he would be better able to ignore them if they hadn't disappeared altogether anyway.

As homework he walked down a street and put himself in scenarios in which the OCD "program" would initiate and that he was to go through a Click Track there and then with his earphones on. He did so with eyes open and to anyone watching it would just look like he was tapping along to music. He did this a few times and his OCD literally disappeared almost overnight. Often a little more work is required with OCD but he seemed to be someone who responded particularly well to the tracks.

We did a similar thing for his gambling addiction which he really wanted to be rid of. Again when we are doing something we know we shouldn't but feel compelled to do so, the compulsion is really just an emotion. By treating it as an emotion and putting it through a Click Track it can quickly lose its grip over us. As well as this strategy we created some behaviour strategies which would massively reduce the risk of him "caving in" in the early

For a personal consultation visit: www.themindhealer.co.uk

days by keeping him away from the computer and coming up with good alternative ways for him to pass his time.

The next and final time I saw him much of his OCD and gambling had massively diminished. However he had a strong belief and fear that he was going to be burned alive and that his mother was going to get cancer. We ran a PSTEC Negative on, "someone close to me is going to die soon" which had a dramatic calming impact on him. This statement was chosen after a deep conversation about his thoughts and feelings and seemed to be the most relevant at this point in time.

We ended with PSTEC Positive statements about him being able to cope with any of life's challenges. I heard from him 6 months later and his OCD and gambling addiction were a thing of the past. He was also feeling calmer and happier.

Miss A - OCD and PSTEC Negative

Miss A's OCD was widespread and almost constant. She couldn't cope with odd numbers; so for example if we placed 5 books together she would feel anxiety until she was able to move one away from the others. She often would say something but then feel very anxious unless she was able to persuade someone to repeat what she had just said.

In my office following the pre-talk, I checked whether she actually believed the catastrophizing that occurs in these scenarios. She said that she knows it is ridiculous but the fear is so real that she feels compelled to act on it. I asked if she'd be

For a personal consultation visit: www.themindhealer.co.uk

able to wind herself up about anything in my office. She saw a few unused plugs which were switched off and said that for some reason it makes her feel very anxious and she wanted to get up and switch them on, even though they weren't in use.

At this point I had already gone through her past and nothing had really stood out. Rather than dig for a cause I decided to experiment working directly on the anxiety/compulsion itself. She was happy to go through a Click Track whilst looking at the plugs to see if she could maintain the 8/10 anxiety she currently felt. One Click Track is all it took and at the end she was unable to bring up any bad feelings. She sat looking at the plugs smiling at the fact that she felt calm. I next sought out another experiment which involved odd numbers. I asked whether if I placed 5 coins on the table in front of her, it would induce any anxiety. She said it would but only if they added up to an odd amount.

I placed the coins on the table and immediately an 8/10 anxiety came up. She came out with an elaborate story about how it was the order in which they were in which was freaking her out, with one of the 50p's being away from the others, all alone. She said that would mean something bad would happen to her when she was aged 50. I quickly checked to see if there had been any "left all alone)" memories but there didn't appear to be. Again one Click Track removed all anxiety and she wasn't able to bring any up once the track had finished about the coins.

After this she felt very calm but claimed that she reckoned she would probably be able to freak herself out if she really thought

For a personal consultation visit: www.themindhealer.co.uk

about it. However, I reminded her that she had just tried and was unable to bring up any anxiety, whereas prior to this it came up within seconds. I also made her realise that anyone can wind themselves up if they try to just by thinking about bad thoughts. I gave her some tasks to carry out at home to clear as much emotion away as possible.

This work would last a few days and then slowly return. It appeared the belief that "I am in danger" was refuelling the emotions and bad patterns. It was also evident that she was quite skilled at negative self-talk. However after running, "I have the belief that I am in danger", through PSTEC Negative, followed up by some PSTEC Positive statements along the lines of "no matter what happens, everything is going to be ok" she felt very different.

She purchased PSTEC Positive extra power and ran through these daily for the next few weeks and had zero OCD during that period or beyond. Regular use of PSTEC Positive is a great way to restructure self-talk so that it works for you, rather than against you.

OCD Summary

I treat OCD in much the same way as I treat most problems. I simply map out what is occurring that the client wants to change. Once they experience the pre-talk and have the best way of

For a personal consultation visit: www.themindhealer.co.uk

viewing the mind in place, we clear any historical pains and then work directly on the symptoms if they persist.

In the cases described here, the people involved knew that the compulsions were irrational despite feeling the fear. Some people need to be gently drawn to a place in which they feel safe to let go of some of their patterns because they actually think there is a real risk of not complying with their compulsions. For these people I might begin by suggesting that if we can lower the emotional intensity of the compulsions, it doesn't mean that they aren't able to follow through with it. If they choose to do so for any reason, they are free to do so with or without a feeling of compulsion. This is similar to bypassing the resistance someone may feel about letting go of anger, by telling them it isn't about forgiveness.

However once the emotion has lifted, they are often able to see the entire situation with much greater clarity and are more open to change. Other people may require some belief change before even getting to that point. There are too many variables to talk about them all but I hope that this has given you food for thought, whether you are a sufferer of OCD or are helping a client.

A common theme within sufferers of OCD is that of their sense of certainty being knocked. The symptoms of their problem could be seen as that of a subconscious mind trying to experience at least some control over their life, even with imaginary dangers.

For a personal consultation visit: www.themindhealer.co.uk

Post-Traumatic Stress - Manchester Arena Terror Attack

Following the awful terrorist attack at the Manchester Arena during the Ariana Grande concert, several schools approached me specifically to work with a large number of children who had been present at the concert. I have worked with people who have endured all sorts of traumas but often there has been quite a time delay between the event occurring and them seeing me. In this case however, a mere day or two had passed since the trauma took place and this was evident in how shook up the children who saw me were.

As you will have noted from many of the case studies described so far, even severe trauma can be worked on directly using the emotion clearing tracks. The longer ago the event, the quicker the emotion is likely to be released. I particularly like using the Click Track 2015 audios due to emphasis on safety throughout the suggestions.

In "PSTEC in the Trenches" I describe some methods which can be used for those who find it too much to focus on the event directly. This included for example, having them think about just one aspect of the trauma such as where it took place, or focusing more on the events leading up to it to begin with rather than the event itself.

For a personal consultation visit: www.themindhealer.co.uk

I found that most of the children found it too upsetting to think about any aspect of what happened that night directly. Although none of them were physically hurt, many had either just been near where the bomb exploded and had to leave early for example, which led to constant "what if" questions. Another boy was in the toilets when it went off and he assumed there was a machine gunman slaughtering people outside where his father was waiting. He was stood on top of the toilet seat hoping they would assume the toilet was empty when they came in. Of course none of this happened but being in such an extreme situation and having those thoughts can have a profound impact on a person.

Similar to grief, when it comes to trauma, different techniques tend to be more effective depending on how long ago the event occurred. Also in the case studies that follow you will see how we are all impacted by trauma differently and some people simply get less overwhelmed than others.

Miss S

Miss S was clearly anxious as a result of the experience she endured. Until this point she had never been an anxious person but now had a constant background anxiety. Three days had passed since the explosion and she was feeling a 6/10 knot of anxiety in her chest.

Because she didn't seem overwhelmed I asked how she would feel thinking about the experience directly and she was ok with this and the anxiety remained at a 6/10. She experienced a standard Click Track but the anxiety remained at a 6/10. Now

For a personal consultation visit: www.themindhealer.co.uk

she was familiar with the tapping process, we tried an EEF which is more powerful. Had she been more familiar with the Click Tracks already I would have gone straight for the Click Track 2015 audios due to their suggestions of safety.

The EEF brought it down one point to a 5/10. Although it was only one point it was a definite reduction. Sadly, because I had so many people to see we only had time for this. I saw her again several days later and the anxiety remained at the slightly lower 5/10. I began this time with the medium Click Track 2015 but surprisingly it remained at a 5/10. Time permitting I may have tried the longer Click Track 2015 audio but given the fact it hadn't budged at all with the previous track, I decided to begin working with beliefs.

Through conversation it became evident that she was holding the belief that both her and her family are in danger. Again, due to extremely limited time scales, I hadn't had the chance to do my usual pre-talk about the nature of beliefs. I did a scaled down version of this and she realised at the logical level at least that although it makes perfect sense that the belief is there given her experience, it is no longer serving a useful purpose.

This understanding and realisation alone brought the anxiety down one point to a 4/10. Given the time I would have ran that belief through PSTEC Negative. However we didn't have that luxury and the fact that she was already feeling a little calmer through conversation, led me to go straight down the PSTEC Positive route.

For a personal consultation visit: www.themindhealer.co.uk

The key concepts which seemed of importance through conversation were safety and certainty for both herself and her family. We tested various statements and settled on, "Me and my family can feel safe because everything is going to be ok" (this resonated more with her than the grammatically correct version of it). We ran this sentence through PSTEC Positive and it brought her anxiety down to a 3/10. Two more listens of it brought down the anxiety to zero.

It is possible that a few more listens of the EEF or Click 2015 may have made a difference. However, given the limited time and the fact that her anxiety came down a little just through conversation, I believed the best way forward was a direct restructuring of the meaning she was giving to the event. This partly involved conversation followed up with the PSTEC Positive statements. I believe the pre-talk about the nature of beliefs plays a big role in how effective PSTEC Positive is, especially in a case such as this in which it may be met with resistance so soon after the tragedy. Moreover I see the conversation and exploration of thinking to be an important part but made much more robust through PSTEC Positive and Negative.

Miss Y, Miss G, Miss T, Miss A - group session

These 4 girls all went to the concert together. They needed help but would only see me on the condition that they all saw me together though I had reservations about doing so. In any scenario which involves others, our internal narration of what is occurring is impacted by the behaviour and actions of others.

This is especially the case in a novel situation such as going through a process like PSTEC.

My main reservation about doing this group work is that if just one person became upset it would likely impact the others experience and interpretation of what just happened. Also each person may require different help.

I advised the girls initially to just think about anything other than the attack whilst trying out a standard Click Track so they could become familiar with it. However one minute in and one of the girls started sobbing uncontrollably. At the start I had already told them that at any point they could stop if they wished or needed to. All of the girls continued and the three girls who weren't sobbing said they felt no change. The girl who had sobbed had a huge release very quickly and felt much calmer. I suspect that the other girls were a bit freaked out by their friend's upset and seemed distracted and only half-heartedly followed the track.

We decided to leave it there but despite anxiety only coming down for the girl who sobbed at the time of the track, a week later all were completely ok. It is impossible to say whether the Click Track had played a role in this or if a little extra time was enough to make them feel calmer. Whatever the reason, the truth is that even if two people experienced the same trauma, the problem within their model of reality may need an entirely different approach. For one it might just require an emotion removal track and for another it may require belief change.

For a personal consultation visit: www.themindhealer.co.uk

All of the girls commented that although they tried to focus on other things, their minds kept being drawn to the event through the Click Track. It is in situations like this that I get some of my best ideas. I suspected this feature of the mind will likely repeat itself with other people who had also been through a recent trauma so as I was waiting for the next girl I wracked my brain for a solution.

Miss M - conceptual dissociation

Miss M had higher anxiety than some of the other people I had seen so far which was a constant 8/10. Thinking about the event directly was too overwhelming. Following the previous experience, I came up with a plan which would potentially allow a person to think about an abstract version of a traumatic event without having to delve too much into the experiential version.

I had Miss M imagine that she wrote on a piece of paper a word or two which represented the trauma. For her and most of the people that followed they simply imagined writing the words "Manchester Arena". I had them then imagine that they folded this imaginary piece of paper and placed it on the table in front of us. Next we ran through Click Tracks whilst focusing on this imaginary piece of paper.

I found that by and large, because at the conceptual level they were focusing on the event itself, their models of reality tended not to be drawn into the actual trauma. In the many people that followed I sometimes used this approach and sometimes had them imagine they were viewing it on a very small screen, which was very blurred and black and white (this is a standard NLP/hypnosis technique). I found that the imaginary piece of paper idea to be more effective at allowing the Click Tracks to work without overwhelm.

Another finding was that once the concept itself had been de-charged using this method, they were then able to think about the event itself directly and either there was no emotion there, or it was greatly reduced and we were able run a Click Track directly on it.

Using this method, Miss M's anxiety came all the way down to zero after one standard Click Track. After this she was unable to generate any fear at all. To increase the chance of this sticking we ran a PSTEC Positive on "My family and I will be ok". Miss M required no further work.

Miss E

Miss E had been plagued by "what if" questions due to the fact that they had made a last minute decision to leave a little early from the place the bomb actually went off. The "what if's", were combined with a 9/10 anxiety knot in her stomach. Like the others, thinking about the event directly was too much. The "what if's" suggested an underlying belief of being in danger. However I wanted to at least attempt to bring down the emotion using the new idea I had come with up involving the imaginary piece of paper.

For a personal consultation visit: www.themindhealer.co.uk

Two Click Tracks later all anxiety had disappeared. We had no further time in that session but I saw her a week later for an update. She felt much calmer but for two days after our first session the "what ifs" continued but didn't really generate much emotion. On the third day they stopped and she had been fine ever since.

I expected to have to do some belief work as well but as can be seen, we are all different and our brains respond differently to different processes. I suspect the fact that she hadn't directly experienced the blast may have helped (she was in an outside corridor) and moreover, perhaps the "what ifs" withered away of their own accord once the fuel of anxiety was removed via the tracks.

Miss I

Miss I thought her mother was being gunned down whilst she was in the toilets. She responded very well to the "imaginary paper" method and it took just a few Click Tracks to bring her anxiety and upset right down.

I saw her soon after and she was still considerably calmer but the London attacks had just occurred and she felt her anxiety rise if anyone talked about it. She also was very jumpy if she heard loud noises or bangs when walking down the school corridor. This was a very common theme amongst the people I helped and was often something we worked on in the second session. She was able to bring up a 4/10 at the thought of a noisy and busy corridor which was cleared with a Click Track. Next we ran a

PSTEC Positive on, "Because I am safe, I can feel calm in busy corridors" which worked very well. In particular, her mind responded well to the presupposition of "because I am safe". Other variations of this sentence didn't have the same impact.

For Miss I and many others I see who aren't likely to have access to PSTEC Positive once they leave me, I have them write out the statement 7 times first thing in the morning and just before bed to reinforce the idea whilst visualising everything getting back to normal.

Miss M

Miss M responded well to the tracks using the imaginary paper method and it took just a few tracks to remove all anxiety. I saw her again a week later and some anxiety had returned but not back to the old levels. Again, her trauma was reinforced because of the London attacks. She felt upset because she didn't feel she could ever feel safe again in a city centre.

To complicate matters further her parents had been on holiday when the attacks took place and they were only returning the following week. We discussed that it is quite normal to have a period of anxiety like this following such an experience. I also explained that if we removed the anxiety again, she could still choose not to visit a city until she felt better and some time had passed.

She agreed that this makes sense and the 6/10 anxiety that was there cleared with one Click Track and she wasn't able to bring back the feeling. We next discussed potential PSTEC Positive statements which included the idea that it is logical to take precautions but that also she could feel safe. The one we settled on was, "despite everything I can feel safe and calm". On paper this seemed perfect but whilst saying it out loud she began sobbing.

This is a key benefit of ending with PSTEC Positive statements as they can sometimes uncover hidden emotions when saying them out loud. We cleared the 8/10 upset which had come up with one Click Track and discussed other potential PSTEC Positive statements which might be more effective for her at this point in time (the previous statement still didn't "feel right"). She settled on, "I can feel safe because things will go back to normal soon", which tested out fine when saying it out loud and had a very positive impact on her. On the surface it doesn't seem much different to the previous statement but our models of reality can be so sensitive to the specific words used as well as their exact order. I also suspect this statement worked because of the word "soon" which reinforced that her parents would be home soon.

Miss P

Miss P had an 8/10 that failed to respond to any of the emotion removing Click Tracks, with or without the imaginary paper method. She had a strongly held belief that she was in imminent danger which she agreed might not be helping. We ran this through PSTEC Negative which removed most of the anxiety and followed it up with a few generic "I am safe" type PSTEC Positive statements which left her feeling calm and happy from that point on. For any trauma or problem that isn't being cleared by the emotion removing tracks, PSTEC Negative and Positive are the best candidates for clearing the problem to cement any new insights obtained through conversation.

Recent Trauma Summary

Again here are a number of case studies which demonstrate the framework in full flow. Even very recent traumas can be cleared quickly with the emotion removing Click Tracks. However, the more recent the event, the more likely you are to have to employ more complex and sophisticated methods. I have since used the imaginary piece of paper with a word or two written on it on numerous occasions and it does an excellent job of allowing someone to connect with a problem without being sucked into the overwhelm.

When that fails to make an impact, consider PSTEC Negatives on any beliefs about being in danger and follow up with PSTEC Positives. As I have discussed throughout this book so far, test different PSTEC Positive options by saying them out loud before going through with it. Once one "feels" right go for it and consider repeating. I personally recommend either doing a PSTEC Positive statement once or twice a day for the following two weeks following a recent trauma or use the writing down method once in the morning and once at night.

For a personal consultation visit: www.themindhealer.co.uk

Until this point I haven't yet tried applying a PSTEC Negative about being in danger as a first port of call in these scenarios. Normally, my aim is to get the emotion as low as possible but I plan to try this out in the near future. I suspect it will work for some and not others but only time will tell.

Complex Cases involving Vulnerable People

Hopefully many of you reading this won't have had to endure some of the tragedies I have discussed so far. In this section I shall describe how I worked through the framework on people with a complex set of emotional difficulties. Many of these people have a very unsettled and unstable home life and have been through horrific experiences, often at the hands of primary caregivers. As a result they suffer from a variety of emotional ills, often with low self-esteem, self-hate and anxiety.

People who have lived through such trauma, tend to have a key emotion which is more prominent than others. In this section I shall be focusing on those who suffer from anxiety. In a future chapter I shall focus on people who have been through similar events but their model of reality has produced anger as a result. Anger is the surface level emotion though, as often underneath this are the more vulnerable emotions such as anxiety and upset.

Miss N - domestic violence, rejection and unresolved grief

At the age of 14, Miss N had experienced far more than many people go through in a lifetime. As a result, she had very low self-esteem and felt anxious and upset most of the time. She had big mood swings and struggled with day to life. Up to the age of 7, she had witnessed almost daily domestic violence from her father towards her mother. At the age of 7 her father told her that he hates her and wished she didn't exist after which she didn't see her father again.

She had lost multiple loved ones including grandparents and aunties/uncles. When she was 12 she witnessed someone being murdered with a sledge hammer. In the 3 months previous to seeing me she had lost another grandparent and split up from her boyfriend. In the past few weeks someone had been sending her mother death threats which the police were taking seriously. The police had suggested they relocate.

Despite everything Miss N was a very bubbly girl, albeit a little volatile and you would never guess on the surface that she had been through so much. This is one of those cases which on paper you would expect it to take many sessions of clearing emotions and unpicking beliefs; however this was not the case.

When multiple traumas are involved I choose one from a long time ago and work my way back to the more recent traumas. Therefore we began clearing the emotions of anger and upset from the early domestic violence memories. Miss N responded extremely well to the Click Tracks and each time we went through it, no matter how high the emotion started off, by the end of the track it disappeared and didn't come back.

For a personal consultation visit: www.themindhealer.co.uk

Next we cleared the upset of rejection from her father which again cleared very quickly. Underneath anger towards her father was self-hate. This can be expected in a situation such as this; children nearly always assume blame for something such as this and often come to the conclusion that they mustn't be lovable, which can result in self-hate. A Click Track cleared the self-hate in one fell swoop and through conversation it seemed that no further restructuring/reframing was required in this area.

Amazingly, one Click Track cleared all trauma from observing the sledgehammer murder at which point we ran out of time. At the start of the session I asked her what was the most painful thing out of everything that she had been through. Her answer was splitting up with her boyfriend. Relationship breakups can be harrowing and she was obviously suffering at the thought of this. However if I'd have targeted that to start with, I suspect all the other pent up trauma may have made clearing more difficult.

The next time I saw her I checked to see if our previous work had remained intact. She was amazed at how much calmer she was feeling and we had to do no further work on those things. Next we focused on unresolved grief. We started on the grief she felt for her auntie who died 7 years previously that was still raw. Clearing this seemed to clear the unresolved grief she felt for all of the other people she had lost. Moreover she also felt calmer when thinking about her ex-boyfriend.

In a sense, a relationship break up is a kind of grieving process. After the track she said that he was a bit of an idiot anyway whilst laughing. Most of the case studies in this piece of work have been focused on when things haven't gone to plan, as this helps to demonstrate how to progress in those scenarios. However this is quite a typical result I achieve in just one or two sessions with many of the people I work with.

I expected to have to make great use of PSTEC Negative and Positive, especially considering the way she had been rejected so awfully by her father. In her model of reality, all of these thoughts must have drifted away when the emotions were cleared. Miss N went from being a very troubled and volatile young girl, to being the real version of her; the bubbly and likable girl she would have been all along had she not had so much bad luck in life.

Miss L - multiple trauma, sexual abuse, rejection, panic attacks, and unresolved grief

Miss L was a teenage girl who had already experienced a life no-one should have to experience. Unlike the previous case, this one is more typical of what might need to be done when there are so many emotional and thinking related problems. Miss L had made multiple suicide attempts in the past (though she wasn't suicidal when she saw me), self-harmed, had numerous panic attacks each day and had years of psychological help including Cognitive Behaviour Therapy and medication with very little improvement.

She had been sexually abused by her father until the age of 6, at which point she was put into care. Two years ago she had been sexually assaulted and six months previously she had been attacked in the city centre and was left badly beaten. As a result, she cannot go anywhere near the city without major panic occurring.

She had been passed around different foster parents but for the last 3 years had been with the same ones who she really liked. Normally I begin work with the earliest event, which in this case involved her father but it was too traumatic to even tell me about, let alone work on in that first session.

As she hadn't experienced PSTEC before, I chose something which caused her some upset and anxiety but which wasn't too overwhelming. Five years ago in primary school she had been bullied, the thought of which brought up anger and upset. She felt comfortable experiencing PSTEC on this and so we ran a Click Track. The emotion was around 7/10 and disappeared after the one listen.

The previous two attacks she had endured in the city centre which seemed to be main cause of her current panic attacks were having a big impact on her life. We agreed that she needed to stay safe but that one can stay safe without constant panic being present. She felt she had made some poor choices on both occasions in terms of being alone, it being quite late at night in an area that wasn't really considered safe. She also felt she had learned from this and would never go out alone again at that time of night.

Once I was happy that removing the fear wasn't putting her in danger we ran a medium length Click Track 2015 which brought her from a shaking panic to complete calm, to her amazement.

For a personal consultation visit: www.themindhealer.co.uk

The session ended and I gave her the task of testing our work. This was quite easy as she passed the area daily on the bus which almost always produced a panic attack.

The next week I saw her and not only had her panic attacks stopped completely but she had been able to go shopping in the centre with her mother during the day. This was something she thought she would never be able to do again.

Given this success I asked how she felt about potentially tackling her early childhood memories involving her father. She began describing some of what had occurred spontaneously which is something that definitely wouldn't have happened the previous week. As she did so, I interrupted to say that she didn't have to but she said that she actually wanted to as she hadn't really told anyone for a very long time.

A kaleidoscope of emotions came up including hatred and anger towards her father, self-hate, repulsion and anxiety. The emotions were high but she felt able to focus on the memories directly without being too overwhelmed. Two medium length Click Track 2015's later all of the emotions had cleared from these early events. At that point she wasn't able to bring up any bad feelings at all.

The following week I checked in with her and everything we had done so far remained intact. However some other things had come to the surface which weren't visible before. She felt a great anger towards her foster mother and sister but had no idea why as this was the first time in her life that she felt part of a family.

She agreed that it would be best if we could remove this and so we successfully cleared it with a Click Track. After doing so she realised that a part of her had been worried in case they had said they didn't want to look after her any more. With the anger gone, she saw the situation with greater clarity and realised through conversation that her situation there was stable; especially so as there had been talk of adoption.

After this once more she felt completely at peace and so we needed to let a little more time pass so we could see if there was anything else we needed to clear. The following week one more thing cropped up which was producing intense upset and anxiety. Her biological nan lived nearby who she was very close to. She was getting very old and although she wasn't suffering from a terminal illness, she was slowly getting worse.

This prompted the belief that she will have a complete breakdown when her nan dies and that she won't be able to cope. By "not being able to cope", given her past serious suicide attempt, I suspected that that mental state may resurface if things were left as they were. I had already explained in detail about the nature of beliefs and thought. I made her aware once more that sometimes a strong expectation can actually cause something to occur which wouldn't otherwise. She agreed that it makes sense to weaken this belief and try some better ones out.

We ran, "I have the belief that I will break down if my nan died" through PSTEC Negative, after which she had the new opinion that although it would likely be very difficult, she would actually cope. Next we discussed various potential PSTEC Positive

For a personal consultation visit: www.themindhealer.co.uk

statements and she settled on, "even though it might be hard, I will cope and make her proud". As she began testing this by saying it out loud an image came to her of her singing in front of a huge crowd. She was an excellent singer and this was something that her nan always praised her for.

This image brought her great comfort and she was feeling very calm and happy after running it through PSTEC Positive. In a sense, this image and thought allowed her to have a connection with her nan whether she was alive or not and I suspect it was this which gave her such comfort. I had several "check in" sessions with her over the following several months and each time she was calm, happy and optimistic about the future.

I could literally fill hundreds of pages of case notes such as this but I feel that the examples given above provide a useful demonstration of the tools and framework in action. Next I'll be talking about anger and all the specific nuances involved with that emotion.

Anger

Although I'll be going through the same framework with anger as I do with every problem, the case studies I shall describe will reinforce the application of the framework and also bring up some nuances particular to anger. In many cases the anger someone feels has little to do with whatever is occurring in the here and now.

A person will feel anger and then look around at what is happening to find out the source of the anger. The conclusion they come to will often be wrong. For example imagine a person is experiencing a lot of stress and feeling under attack at work for some reason and next they get home and their spouse asks if they have done a certain chore. Because they are carrying around a lot of stress and anger, their emotional response to this "additional stressor" will likely be much more than is warranted.

A person in this state wouldn't just think that the way they feel is just because of work. The trigger will often be misinterpreted as the actual cause, creating an anger response. I see this kind of thinking error constantly when a person is in a volatile state. Think back to the beginning of the book where I described the

For a personal consultation visit: www.themindhealer.co.uk

boy who had been badly beaten by his father years ago. He too was incorrectly attributing how he was feeling now to current occurrences, despite them playing only a tiny role in the grand scheme of things.

Like anxiety, anger is another survival emotion and as such, our brains are often reluctant to let go of it for fear that we will be in danger. Anger very often forms part of an emotional pyramid. An emotional pyramid is a situation in which one emotion sits on top of another (Tim Phizackerley first described this in PSTEC Advanced Part 1). In my experience anger normally sits on top of the pyramid, underneath which upset often resides. Anxiety is sometimes part of the mix but I find that upset is normally the other side of the coin to anger.

Whether the anger is part of an emotional pyramid or a single emotion within the model of reality depends on the cause. Whereas the basic human need of certainty is often playing a role in anxiety, anger can sometimes fulfil another one of our basic needs as well; that of significance.

One person might simply have had angry parents, which has then become their style of communication. Another person may have been through some kind of bad experience in which anger was required but then, years later, it remains there in the background impacting their day to day life. Yet another person may not feel like they have much going for them and the only way they can feel special or significant is through the vehicle of anger.

For a personal consultation visit: www.themindhealer.co.uk

As you will see in the upcoming examples, an upsetting event can often be a key cause of anger which may seem counterintuitive on the surface. The reason for this is that the anger can give a false sense of certainty and control in situations in which they feel those are lacking. Also many people find anger easier to deal with directly than upset. Having this background knowledge and conveying it in the pre-talk can really help to break down barriers and resistance to letting go of anger.

Miss G - anger at teacher

Miss G had been calm and happy but in recent months was increasingly becoming angry and bad tempered. Not much detective work was required here. She had had a few run-ins with her maths teacher at the beginning of term and their relationship had deteriorated rapidly from that point. I asked how angry she felt on a scale of 1 to 10 when thinking about the teacher. She stared ahead and didn't answer me.

I had no idea what was going on until she started shaking and managed to blurt out that she was raging just at the thought of the teacher. It was clear that she felt a 10/10 anger just at the thought of him. Prior to this in the pre-talk, I had already made a key distinction which I make to all people who experience anger towards a specific person. I explain that removing the anger doesn't mean that they are forgiven. In fact I suggest that they can think whatever they want about the other person but that it would benefit them if they felt calmer.

With the boy I talked about at the beginning of the book whose father had hurt him, he was extremely reluctant to let go of the anger initially. However, as above, I first suggested that it isn't about forgiveness and that he can think what he wants about his father. Next I explained that when it comes to anger, in many cases we are generating the bad feeling and firing it at an image or idea we have of that person in our minds. The other person sometimes never receives any of the intended punishment so in a sense, in those situations we are generating the anger and simply experiencing it ourselves. It's a bit like punching ourselves in the face.

Think back to the castle metaphor of the mind. This anger pre-talk performs an excellent job of persuading the guards and castle staff that we are on their side. This makes any kind of resistance to letting go far less likely. This is very important with anger in particular, as often it can sometimes increase in intensity during a Click Track otherwise.

One standard Click Track removed all anger from Miss G about the teacher. I asked her to try and bring back the anger once the track had finished and she was unable to. Now she was in a place of clarity I set about giving her different potential ways of viewing the situation. I asked her if she chose the anger towards her teacher or if it happened automatically.

People often don't consider the automaticity of their anger and once they realise that, it is easy to apply that to the other person. In other words, it demonstrates that to some extent we are all just being pushed around by emotions that we aren't choosing.

For a personal consultation visit: www.themindhealer.co.uk

We discussed how the conflict first arose and it began as a misunderstanding which then slowly escalated.

Once even a minor conflict arises, there is the chance that the guards in each person's model of reality will be on high alert as they are on the lookout for a potential attack. The higher the guards are on alert, the less likely that any information will pass through to their inner castle. Unfortunately, in many conflicts both parties feel under attack and subsequently the interaction mostly involves firing shots at the other and any useful information that might be conveyed doesn't make it through.

However, once just one of the parties involved in the conflict has had their anger removed through something such as a Click Track as in this case, in a sense, that person's guards become more relaxed. In any future interactions the other person's "guards" will pick up on this change and be more open to properly analysing and potentially accepting incoming information.

I often capitalize on this new state of affairs by first rewriting what has happened and then giving the client a specific task to carry out. In this case we discussed the initial misunderstanding which involved the teacher asking Miss G to do something which she didn't hear and then he shouted at her.

I advised that it is irrelevant who is right and who is wrong and that we should focus on achieving the outcome of a better "working relationship". I asked if this particular teacher is normally aggressive in this way. She admitted that he does seem to be now with her in particular but before that incident they got on well. It then became clear that shortly after this, Miss G had purposefully begun arriving late for class and so the battle commenced.

In schools in particular, I always explain to the pupils that teachers are actual human beings. They can have all sorts of stress, anger and upset going on behind the scenes that the pupil might not have a clue about. I said that for all she knew he had just split up with his wife or lost a loved one. Whatever the reason it appeared he was having a bad day. It is very rare for a child to have already considered that the teachers might also struggle with things so this new perspective can be useful.

She accepted this and that she had added fuel to the fire by purposefully being late. Once conflict like this begins and two people are carrying around anger for someone, I often describe it as not being an authentic interaction. By this, I mean that a person experiencing anger isn't the same as that same person in a place of calm, which I consider a truer reflection of who they are. It's more like an otherwise passive animal becoming aggressive because it is in pain or feels under attack.

I suggested to Miss G that she visit the teacher in question and, whilst in a place of calm, simply ask if they could have a fresh start. She squirmed initially at the thought of this but agreed to do it as soon as the session finished. If she had done this prior to the removal of the anger it wouldn't have worked nor would she have been able to do it. However, now she was calm and was planning to convey a desire to improve the situation, the likelihood of the teacher's model of reality processing and accepting this new information would be considerably improved.

I saw her a few weeks later and not only had the relationship considerably improved but this teacher was now one of her favourite teachers. This combination of removing anger, giving new perspectives on anger, having them become outcome focused and giving them a task which involves conveying new information from a place of calm to the other person, often has a magical impact. You would literally not believe how quickly long standing conflicts have been removed in minutes with this exact method. There will be a separate chapter on communication skills which will delve much deeper into this topic.

Mr L - anger as a temporary tool

Mr L was in an awful situation. He was very intelligent and mature for his 15 years of age and his parents were both heroin addicts. He was having major difficulties with his foster parents and wasn't able to see his younger siblings which he was finding very distressing as he knew they would feel lonely and scared.

He was feeling major anger towards his parents because of the predicament and even though he wasn't seeing them much he would often punch walls just at the thought of them. He had previously experienced Click Tracks with great effect and knew they may help.

We discussed his situation and I gave him some useful ways of thinking about his parents. For example, no-one actually sits

For a personal consultation visit: www.themindhealer.co.uk

down one day and decides they would like to become a heroin addict. However, in this instance he decided to keep the anger. With all of the uncertainty and lack of control, he felt the anger was helping him stay afloat. He asked if he could see me in a month's time and, depending on the situation, he may want to turn down the anger.

For various reasons I wasn't able to see him again but this case study offers a valuable lesson. Although, in most cases, removal of a bad emotion is by far the best thing to do, ultimately the decision is up to the client and occasionally there may be some times when keeping hold of it can be of some use. I suspect I could have used the belief change tracks to embed that sense of certainty without needing the anger but I honoured his decision.

Miss M - unexpected anger towards mother

Over the past 12 months Miss M had begun to feel an increasing anger towards her mother and she had no idea why. Just the sound of her voice created an emotional response in her. Nothing historical seemed to have any relevance and she wasn't an angry person otherwise. In fact she felt guilt at the anger she was feeling which then turned into anger towards herself.

To begin with I had her focus on her mother and bring up the anger. An 8/10 anger resulted but when we tried a Click Track and tapping Accelerator the anger actually increased. This is occurs occasionally and suggests that the subconscious mind has some kind of reason to keep hold of the anger which needs to be looked at.

For a personal consultation visit: www.themindhealer.co.uk

I had the option to have her say out loud, "It is safe to let go of my anger towards mother" to check for subconscious resistance around the idea of safety. If some did arise I would have analysed it and perhaps ran PSTEC Negatives and Positives to overcome this at the belief level. However, she was a confident adult who had had a great relationship with her mother until recently.

She had begun a new stressful job at around the time that the anger began to increase but she was happy in her job now and wasn't able to bring up any stress thinking back to those early days there.

In most situations there are many routes one can take but on this occasion I decided to use a Cascade Release audio track. These tracks work slightly differently from the usual emotional clearing Click Tracks and during it the emotion is focused on rather than any specific event or scenario. She focused on the anger she was feeling and followed the instructions. At the end of the process she said that she felt calmer than she had ever felt in her entire life. All anger towards her mother had gone and didn't return. Why was this? It is impossible to say for sure. The more complex case studies I have already described should have given you an idea of how interlinked memories, experiences and beliefs can be in the model of reality. It could be that her mother had said something in the past when she was embarking on something new and stressful which made her feel worse. The important thing of course is that the problem is now gone and it is another demonstration of how and when Cascade Release can be used to great effect.

For a personal consultation visit: www.themindhealer.co.uk

Miss N and Miss P - group session and increased anger

I was once giving a presentation to a large number of staff at a school and they asked me if they could experience the process. There are a few problems with people experiencing as a group, especially for the first time. I don't want anyone to get very upset as it isn't practical to do any further personal work there and then, so it made sense for them to think of something mildly unpleasant. In particular I asked them to think of something that brings up a definite but small bad feeling somewhere in their body that they would be happy to get rid of so that they can at least get a before and after reading, if needed.

With the four girls I worked with as a group who had experienced a terror attack, each of them probably had a different construction of the problem within their model of reality. This, coupled with it being a new experience, leads people to look for social cues as to how to act and behave, which in turn can lead to a situation in which it is easy for the process to go awry.

This problem is made much worse with a larger group of people. Each person has their own unique problem and as such I am not able to tailor a specific pre-talk to minimize the chance of resistance. Also it is common for people to experience scepticism when they first hear about a tool like PSTEC because it sounds too good to be true. This can lead to people searching for evidence to confirm their existing suspicions rather than just following the instructions.

For a personal consultation visit: www.themindhealer.co.uk

At the beginning of the track a sea of doubtful eyes looked at me and at the end little appeared to have changed. One man said that he focused on something that made him angry and that he started to become even angrier at the voice on the track. This is actually quite common. What is often occurring if ever you hear someone say this or experience it yourself, is that there is a part which doesn't want to let go of the anger and therefore creates anger at the track. I obviously didn't have much time in the middle of a presentation to go into detail with each person, but I asked if they were sure they wanted to let go of the anger. After a little thought he said, "No, actually she deserves it!"

My anger pre-talk described earlier would have reframed anger in multiple ways to reduce/remove resistance before doing the Click Track but this hadn't been possible in this instance. Another person had anxiety turn into anger. This is less common and a quick discussion revealed that his religious beliefs led him to feel that it wasn't right to remove an emotional pain that God had put there. Given the chance for a pre-talk or further individual work then and there, we could have analysed this and I suspect I could have given him better viewpoints which would have allowed the pain to disappear whilst not clashing with his religious beliefs.

I asked how everyone else had found it and a few non-committal shrugs was the response. Thankfully, by this point I had already had a great deal of success with therapy and PSTEC in various environments and confidently told them that a group setting wasn't ideal, and to judge my work on the impact of my one on one work with the kids.

At the end when everyone else had left, about 10 people came up to me saying how profoundly it had impacted them. This is a clear demonstration of the social dynamics involved in a new situation for which there are no predetermined cues. People simply look to others for guidance on how to behave and because the first two people to respond gave negative feedback, they decided not to say anything. I suspect that, if the people who had had a more profound impact had been more vocal to start with, the overall feeling in the room would have been different.

Mr J and Mr Q -major anger towards a parent

For many people who have anger towards a specific person, there is normally a build-up of relatively minor things over time which results in anger. Without any further complications, as with the girl who had anger at the teacher, a simple Click Track or two will suffice.

Mr J had had a huge argument with his mother, which had become physical and nearly resulted in them both falling over a balcony and down some stairs. Mr J was furious at this and other events involving his mother and felt hatred and major anger towards her as a result. He decided to move in with his father and was happier there but if ever he got a text or heard from his mother, he would be very on edge and volatile for the rest of the day.

Following my anger pre-talk he agreed that it would benefit him if he felt less anger day to day and if it wasn't triggered so easily.

For a personal consultation visit: www.themindhealer.co.uk

Two Click Tracks cleared all anger and although he had no desire to have his mother back in his life, he felt much better. She had texted him a few times and the following week his anger had returned.

In this case it was a simple case of reapplying the Click Track which then permanently removed the anger. I considered working at the belief level but we had very limited time in that session, so to calm him down in the moment I decided on the Click Track. Sometimes all that is needed is a little more standard Click Track to make the change permanent.

Contrast this with Mr Q. He also had major anger at his mother who had kicked him out of his house a few months previously and so he was couch surfing on various friends' sofas. Click Tracks seemed to rapidly increase the anger he was feeling towards his mother. A Cascade Release whilst focusing on the anger alone (rather than his mother who is the object of his anger) also made his anger increase. Although it didn't help in this scenario, use of Cascade Release in these situations often does work and so should be considered a potential option in these scenarios.

Sadly Mr Q moved schools before I had chance to do further work with him. Had I been given the chance, my focus would have been more at the belief/concept level, checking for potential subconscious resistance to letting go of the anger and removing it with the belief change tracks such as PSTEC Positive and Negative. I would also have considered using the "imaginary writing down" method that I described in the section on the

For a personal consultation visit: www.themindhealer.co.uk

Manchester Arena Terror Attack. In other words, he may have just imagined writing down his mother's name on a piece of paper, folding it and then running an emotion clearing Click Track on that.

Mr Z - anger towards women

Mr Z was escorted to me by the police and wasn't allowed to come into contact with any women. If he was near any women he would feel a rage and there was serious risk of violence and in the past he had threatened them with knives.

He had major anger in general but with males there had to be a trigger, whereas with women no trigger was required. A quick trawl through his history revealed a life moving from care home to care home. Despite major tragedy, he said he felt calm and was numb to all that had happened.

He had no idea why he felt so angry towards women but equally felt that they brought it on themselves. He wasn't able to bring up any anger on demand. Whilst trawling through his history some very extreme experiences in the first few years of his life came up. At the age of 3, he had witnessed his father murder his baby sister in front of him.

To make an already unimaginable situation worse, once his father was sent to prison, his mother abandoned him. Despite the severity of these scenarios he said he felt numb to all of that.

For a personal consultation visit: www.themindhealer.co.uk

With all the information to hand, I began explaining the nature of beliefs/reality/emotions. I explained that concepts and ideas formed very early in life often have a habit of overgeneralising. For example, as I mentioned in PSTEC Advanced Part 2, if a 3 year old is bitten by a dog, initially they may be fearful of just that particular type of dog. However it is quite common for the fear to begin spreading to other similar "concepts" as the model of reality develops. So the child over time may become scared of all breeds of dog no matter what their size is or how placid they are.

I then suggested a potential theory as to why he has so much anger towards women. I suggested that as a very small child, the female who is supposed to be his primary caregiver abandoned him straight after a major trauma. It could be that his young mind over time came to distrust women in general as they can hurt and reject you, all based upon the actions of one woman many years ago.

As I was talking he was looking a little dazed, almost as if he was in a conversational trance. I then offered as an alternative that in the world we are all unique. Most people are good people but you get some people of both sexes who could potentially hurt and reject you. We then discussed the pros and cons of adopting new beliefs based on this fresh understanding.

He was very confused yet willing to run a PSTEC Negative on, "I have the belief that all women will hurt me". This was followed by a PSTEC Positive on "From now on I can feel calm around women". He looked visually different following this

For a personal consultation visit: www.themindhealer.co.uk

combination of tracks and acknowledged that, although confused he does feel very different.

This is one of those very frustrating cases in which, due to circumstances I wasn't able to see him again as he was leaving the area soon after. However I am certain that the work we did will have made an impact on that one area, given his initial response. I am equally certain that he would need much more work to get to a point in which he was able to deal with day to day life in a more confident and calm manner, given what he had been through.

This is a great example of how anger can sometimes be removed via some detective work, followed by belief change. Mr Q in the last example, who became angrier when going through either the Cascade Release or Click Tracks whilst thinking about his mother, would likely have benefited from this approach.

Anger and Unresolved Grief

I alluded earlier to the idea that anger and upset are often two sides of the same coin. In working with clients, once I have ruled out obvious causes of anger such as historical bullying/violence, I will seek out other traumas which may otherwise seem unrelated. I have found that unresolved grief, even from years ago is quite a common cause of anger and often the person is completely unaware of this.

For a personal consultation visit: www.themindhealer.co.uk

Miss L - bad temper

Miss L was becoming angry at herself because she often snapped at loved ones when it wasn't justified. She was also angry at work and was often accused of being very confrontational. She described a background feeling of being on edge which she had had for as long as she could remember.

We trawled through her past and nothing of obvious note came to light. At the end of checking for the usual culprits such as whether they have been bullied, been in an accident, suffered a bereavement etc. I always ask if there is anything else in their life which either has or which is causing them emotional pain. She mentioned that she was a twin but her sister had died during birth, then she went on to mention one or two other things but none of it seemed particularly significant on paper or emotionally.

She said that she does think about her sister occasionally but it was decades ago and with her dying so young she hadn't had the opportunity to "know" her. As a test, I had her focus on her sister and the idea of her twin not being here. There was nothing at first then a flood of tears came out to her major surprise. Two Click Tracks cleared this and all upset had gone.

I theorised that although it makes no logical sense, perhaps a part of her blamed her sister for not making it and being there for her as a sister. I suggested this possibility to see if it resonated and after a few minutes of silence major anger had surfaced along

For a personal consultation visit: www.themindhealer.co.uk

with major guilt. She was stunned and said that it actually did feel as though that were true.

We cleared this anger with a Click Track and she felt considerably lighter. I heard many months later that the background aggro seemed to be a thing of the past and she was much happier both in work and at home.

This exact scenario I have come across on numerous occasions. Sometimes you need to adopt the simple pattern matching and protection mindset that the subconscious mind employs when figuring out what incorrect conclusions it has arrived at. Next, run this mindset through the various experiences a person has been through and see if you can figure how concepts may have been warped and misconfigured. Once you have a potential theory, see if it resonates with the client or yourself and depending on the outcome, consider using the belief change or emotion clearing tracks.

Mr K - Oppositional Defiant Disorder (ODD) Case 1

ODD is a relatively new diagnosis that psychologists have created and is being applied to many people, especially school children. Treatment generally takes several months and consists of multiple types of psychotherapy and medication as it often coincides with a diagnosis of ADHD also. Symptoms included being very angry and defiant with more than just the immediate family; it needs to last more than 6 months and cause significant problems at school or work.

I prefer to dismiss the labels initially and figure out exactly what is going on to start with. He was very reluctant to go along with anything anyone said both at school and at home. He had been diagnosed several years ago with ODD but nothing seemed to be changing.

I began my usual historical fact finding mission and identified that 10 years previously when Mr K was just 4 years old, his grandfather died. I asked if it still felt raw even though it was a long time ago and Mr K became very upset. I applied the pre-talk I described in the chapter on grief and ran the pain through a Click Track.

He felt much calmer and wasn't able to bring up anger or upset about anything at that point in time. We checked and there didn't appear to be any other pockets of emotional pain and he said normally he'd quite easily be able to generate anger towards specific teachers.

In this instance, the session lasted for just 20 minutes including the Click Track and years of ODD disappeared without a trace, whereas all other help had failed. By no means would I predict this would always be the case but sometimes PSTEC allows for solutions which aren't otherwise possible. This is another example of why it can be a good idea to clear all historical pain before working on specific current problems because many problems simply evaporate once the emotion is released.

For a personal consultation visit: www.themindhealer.co.uk

Mr U - ODD Case 2

Mr U had been suffering from quite severe ODD in the last few years. He just felt that he struggled to be told what to do and felt on edge much of the time. A quick analysis revealed that 3 years ago his grandfather passed away. However, there were some specific factors involved which made complete sense as to why a subconscious mind might begin ODD type traits.

His grandfather was looking very ill and Mr U wanted to visit him. Although he looked very ill he was expected to make a full recovery and so his parents said that he couldn't visit him yet and to give it a bit more time as they didn't want him to see his grandfather looking as he did. Obviously his parents were looking out for Mr U and up until that point Mr U had never considered this. Sadly his grandfather took an unexpected turn for the worse and passed away.

Let's examine this from a subconscious point of view. Mr U wanted to do something which figures of authority (his parents) didn't allow and as a result major pain resulted. It makes sense that a simplistic subconscious mind whose mode of operation is that of simple pattern matching and protection from pain, might come to the incorrect conclusion that the pain was caused by authority figures who wouldn't let him do what he wanted to do.

The subconscious mind partly uses emotions to guide behaviour and so if a person deemed to be an authority figure gives an order, in this instance it creates anger as a way of preventing the possibility of pain. Of course from a logical perspective, this is all

For a personal consultation visit: www.themindhealer.co.uk

ridiculous but the subconscious mind doesn't work at the level of logic.

Thinking about his grandfather brought up a lot of anger and upset which he wanted to turn down if possible. A few Click Tracks left him feeling much better. We then discussed particular problem lessons and there were one or two teachers for whom he could generate some anger. We cleared the anger and reframed the interactions they were having, in order to increase the chance that they could improve their relationship. Children often bring out a maturity that wouldn't otherwise be there when they are spoken to like this, made to be part of the solution and also told that to a large extent they aren't to blame for the conclusions their subconscious minds came to. This makes it far more likely that they will follow my instructions and complete our work, by choosing to approach the teachers with whom they have problems in an effort to improve the situation. I suspect the teachers involved are often very surprised when an otherwise childish and seemingly unruly child all of a sudden approaches them and communicates in a way that even many adults probably wouldn't.

Mr U's behaviour improved significantly in the month following but beyond that I have no information as I wasn't able to see him again.

Miss J - complex anger, significance and a sense of identity
Whether you are a self-helper or a therapist, even though you are far less likely to come across extreme cases like the one I shall

For a personal consultation visit: www.themindhealer.co.uk

now describe, I believe the inclusion of these types of examples are a great learning tool. Certain key ideas and methods can be harnessed for simpler cases involving anger or even other psychological pains.

Like many of the people in this book, Miss J had had a very rough time in her 14 years of life so far. She had received years of regular counselling, psychotherapy and medication following multiple suicide attempts and self-harm. When I first saw her she was having several mini breakdowns a week in which he sobbed and shook uncontrollably for hours.

She had been adopted at about the age of 7 years old, prior to which she had endured years of sexual and physical abuse by her father. She had suffered severe bullying throughout primary school and suffered many other traumas since then.

When a person has been through so much, I will often choose one of the less significant events to start with to ease them into it. We began with anger and upset about the primary school bullying which was a 6/10. She could have gotten it much higher but we agreed it might be best to leave it at that level to start with. Throughout the Click Track she was yawning which is always a good sign that release is occurring. At the end she rated the feeling at about 5/10 but was obviously much more relaxed and seemed quite giddy. I asked if she could bring back the one point of anger she had lost but she laughed nervously when she couldn't.

For a personal consultation visit: www.themindhealer.co.uk

She said, "I can't believe it worked! How can just tapping do that!". She agreed that it might be worthwhile working on the more significant and troubled events in her life the next time. When she arrived for session two she began talking and literally didn't stop for a full 50 minutes whilst looking at the clock and said she was too tired to do any Click Tracks. At the end I told her that she had spent many years talking about her problems but this hadn't helped her much and that for change to occur she must do the Click Tracks. She agreed that she would do it the next time.

In session 3 she stormed into my office and said, "There is no way I am doing a Click Track I'm in a bad mood and it's annoying". Conversation had previously revealed that although she was carrying major upset and anxiety, anger was by far the most dominant emotion. Apparently she had a reputation where she lived and often got into fights.

With less experience of PSTEC and how our minds worked, I may have incorrectly come to the conclusion that maybe PSTEC wasn't gelling with her or that she just didn't really want help. However, this is a very common pattern and I asked her to say out loud, "I can be safe without anger". She scoffed at the ridiculousness of this statement which confirmed that her subconscious mind considered letting go of it a threat.

Previous conversations with her had also revealed to me that she achieved her sense of significance from her anger as many of her peers feared her. Moreover, although her adopted parents gave her everything she needed, she felt as though she never received

- 234 -

the attention she required and it appeared that her anger at home was a way of forcing attention to be focused on her.

Because these patterns had gone on for years, they had formed part of her identity. It is common for people to be very fearful of making a big change to their identity, especially when a core part of it is an emotion. They worry about who they will be without the anger for example, and how they will act and be with the change. Therefore it was my job to tackle this resistance with the hope of encouraging her to move forward with the Click Tracks.

I had already explained how the mind works, the nature of beliefs and emotions to pave the way for additional conversations. Next we discussed the idea of anger and safety. My aim was to make her realise that she would actually be safer without the anger. She had already told me multiple stories in which she was overly aggressive towards people and I suggested that being this way actually put her in far riskier situations than she would otherwise be in.

Then I countered the typical belief in people such as her; that just because the background anger is reduced, it doesn't mean that she won't be able to become angry if it is actually required. I told her that it would just be less likely to fire off randomly and when it isn't warranted.

Regarding her fear of a big identity level change, I explained that we can take baby steps to ease her into feeling calm. I also suggested that if at any point she decided that feeling calm wasn't for her, we could use PSTEC Positive to bring back the anger.

For a personal consultation visit: www.themindhealer.co.uk

Finally we discussed the sense of significance she achieved through the vehicle of anger. I told her that her reputation wouldn't just disappear overnight and that some people might actually be a bit unnerved when they see her calmer and more in control. I could have gone through different ways in which she could achieve that significance but I decided to take the path of least resistance to start with. In terms of attention at home I gave her some communications and interpersonal relationship advice which she could use to obtain a healthier relationship with her mother.

This talk led her to being more open to going ahead with the tracks. She had a lot of anger towards her adopted father which had built up over many years. He had said many hurtful things towards her and she felt a rage just thinking about him. We ran a Click Track on the 10/10 anger she had towards him after which she said, "I hate you...how does that work!? I can't believe it actually worked!" She repeatedly jested that she hates me and said that this is the first time anything has actually helped. In fact she said that the 10 minutes of the Click Track had done more for her than many years of therapy. Her relationship with her adopted father improved dramatically and the mutual dislike for each other shifted without any further work done on that part of her life.

The following week she plucked up the courage to work on the historical abuse she received at the hands of her father which brought a 10/10 anger and upset. As she was already familiar with the Click Tracks we went straight for an EEF track which cleared it in one listen. She also told me that people still seem to give her respect even when she isn't angry and aggressive and she is getting used to the new found calm she was feeling.

I had more work to do with Miss J and in the weeks following we worked on her self-esteem and if any anger cropped up we came up with better ways to think of it. We also created new behaviours and habits which would increase the chance that she got on with people better. She found that now she was calmer her parents were giving her much more attention and the old strategy of having to use anger for attention became a thing of the past.

Yet again the raw power of PSTEC can be seen in action, creating change in a person after the first listen. This case also shines a light on potential areas of subconscious resistance in the form of secondary gain that anger can bring such as respect/wariness, significance and attention. The idea of actually being safer when calm had to be introduced, which has parallels in anxiety. On this occasion I managed to obtain full agreement through a quick conversation but, had resistance surfaced whilst going through the tracks, I would have considered running the idea of anger meaning safety through PSTEC Negative and the opposite through PSTEC Positive.

Finally it also demonstrated the idea that if an emotion has been present with someone for a long time, even if it is bad, the idea of letting it go can feel very scary. The fear of the unknown is often greater than putting up with the misery of carrying around the emotion. We can bypass resistance in this area by having the person realise that they will still have access to the emotion when

For a personal consultation visit: www.themindhealer.co.uk

it is actually needed and that in the unlikely event that it is really missed, it could be brought back through PSTEC Positive.

Anger and concept restructure

Mr M

Mr M had major anger but was responding extremely well to the standard Click Tracks. Using those tracks we blasted through a ton of traumas throughout his life and he felt immeasurably better as a result. One niggle remained though; if he felt that a situation was unfair, his brain would produce intense anger which would take over his mind and would result in an outburst. Afterwards, he would then feel great regret over his actions and would feel guilt and self-directed anger.

We ran a Click Track on specific recent instances in which this pattern had occurred and the anger disappeared. However, unlike all of the other clearances we had made, this one resurfaced the moment "unfairness" presented itself again. By this point he had already had my pre-talk and was keen to respond in different ways in these scenarios if he could.

For Mr M, "unfairness" purely involved him getting into trouble for something that he didn't do. He also had embedded within his mind the idea that unfairness should always be punished. To begin with, we analysed exactly what occurs in class. He admitted that he often acts childish to which I suggested that from a teacher's perspective, if someone often "messes about" and then something happens in which it isn't clear exactly who has done something, they are more likely to assume it is the person who has a reputation. He agreed that this made sense.

Next I made him aware that teachers jobs are very stressful, they are under major pressure for their classes to achieve certain grades, so when people do act up it can create a lot of stress. He hadn't thought of this before. I then put forth the idea that unfairness is just a mistake. A big light bulb appeared to go off in his head at this thought. I wasn't going to be able to see Mr M for a while so to increase the chance lasting change occurring, we ran "I have the belief that unfairness should be punished" through PSTEC Negative. We then followed this up after some testing, with a PSTEC Positive on, "unfairness is often just a mistake". Months later I found out that this restructure had remained in place and he was doing much better in school as a result.

Here is a clear example of using PSTEC Negative and Positive to undo anger which hasn't responded to the usual emotion clearing tracks. Prior to this, I spent a little time preparing his "castle" via the belief change pre-talk. This is common tactic I use to create the best chance of the tracks working with little to no resistance. In one of the previous case studies in which the boy felt a rage towards his mother which wasn't helped by Click Tracks or Cascade Release, I would likely have pursued some version of this strategy.

Mr E - anger & conceptual reframe without using any tracks

Mr E was very quick to anger and it went from 0-10 almost immediately. He was never able to bring up any anger on demand and if he saw me when he was in an agitated state, it did calm him down but didn't make any lasting impact on him.

Initially we identified key problem areas/times in which flare ups occurred and then we came up with behavioural solutions to try out. For example, every morning was a flash point as he was often running late for school and he would battle with his mother as a result and therefore start every day in a bad mood. Sometimes it can take someone outside of a situation to come up with an obvious solution and I suggested that he get up 15 minutes earlier. This would result in no rush, no arguments with his mother and therefore his anger would be less likely to flare up whilst at school. He agreed that this made perfect sense and he began the following day and it made a huge impact.

We created several more solutions to such problems and with each one implemented, the number of times per week in which he had an outburst gradually shrunk to just once or twice. There was one particular program in his mind which took over in certain scenarios and would lead him to behave in a way which he would later regret. It often involved him breaking a small rule and then responding stubbornly. For example, they aren't allowed to use phones in class but he received an emergency text. However, because he got his phone out, he got into trouble with his teacher which led to a big argument.

For a personal consultation visit: www.themindhealer.co.uk

He didn't want to continue this pattern but it seemed lodged in place. A very small minority of people prefer not to do the Click Tracks. For some it might be boredom, for others it's too much effort even though just 10 minutes of it can result in lasting change. Mr E had his reasons but he didn't want to focus on PSTEC. I considered using the characters approach as described in PSTEC Advanced Part 2 which would have helped dissociate him from his thought process, increase self-awareness and therefore give him more control over them.

However, I decided to dig deeper to see if there were any resources we could work with. When Mr E had one of these moments, he would literally sacrifice everything with his stubbornness. For example, he would rather be excluded from school completely than hand his phone over. When Mr E was in the middle of experiencing anger, it was clear that changing for his own benefit wasn't a very effective motivator of change. Further conversation revealed that he had a very good relationship with the head teacher.

He had fallen behind with his studies and the head teacher had given up a lot of his own personal time to help him catch up. I attempted to build up this internal resource by explaining how rare it is for a head teacher to go to so much trouble to help one child. Mr E had appreciated the help he was getting but hadn't fully realised how good of the head teacher this was, and as a result his gratitude increased.

Next I tested to see if we could use this as leverage within his model of reality. I suggested to him that when one of these

For a personal consultation visit: www.themindhealer.co.uk

scenarios arises, not only is he jeopardizing his own future but in a sense he is also throwing away all of the many hours that the head teacher had invested to help him out. The addition of his behaviour impacting someone he was grateful to seemed to make a big difference to Mr E in terms of motivation to change.

Once it was clear this internal resource was one that could be used, I advised that whenever a similar situation arose, he was to imagine that he was literally throwing away dozens of hours of the head teacher's life. He thought about this and sensed that it may make a difference even if he was feeling stubborn. This was a school which I only visited once every 3-4 months and so we didn't have the luxury of building on this work. However I later found out that although other problems still remained, this particular issue which was a regular occurrence hadn't happened since our session.

This is a very powerful cognitive technique which can be used in conjunction with PSTEC or instead of, when PSTEC isn't suitable or available for any reason. It is just a case of having a general conversation to see what their interests are, who they like, what they like doing etc. Be on the lookout for things which can potentially be leveraged or reframed.

For a personal consultation visit: www.themindhealer.co.uk

Anger and Internal Resources

Mr H - song lyric as an internal resource

Mr H was being bullied which produced instant and excessive anger. He didn't respond to any of the usual PSTEC techniques even though he was able to bring up the anger. EEF's, Click Track 2015 and Cascade Release didn't budge it one bit. PSTEC Negative wasn't available at the time.

In situations such as these, one thing I am on the lookout for are potential behavioural changes which can be carried out. For example it could be that he was only bullied in a particular area at a particular time and might have just been a case of avoiding these scenarios.

At the same time, I am also on the lookout for potential resources - both inner and outer which may be utilised. I often ask what their interests are and in particular who they admire. Mr H was a huge Bob Marley fan and I asked him if he thought Bob Marley would get so stressed at these immature boys if he were in that situation. In reply he came out with an obscure lyric from one of his tunes and after saying it he burst into laughter.

I can't remember the exact lyric right now but I remember thinking that it wouldn't resonate with most people. However, the impact of it on his model of reality was definite and that is the most important thing. I suggested he run it through PSTEC Positive whilst at the same time imagining him responding in the problem scenarios in a way that he thought Bob Marley might respond. Afterwards he thought about the lads who had been

For a personal consultation visit: www.themindhealer.co.uk

bothering him and whereas before he got agitated, now he just laughed and wondered why he had been so bothered in the first place.

He had other issues to be dealt with but this is a good example of seeking out resources they already have within their model of reality and ramping up the power of certain key ideas/viewpoints. If you can find someone they admire and ask them what they would say/think/do in the problem context, it can reliably make a big dent on the presenting problem.

Psychopathy

Mr L - suspected psychopath

This was a very frustrating case in that I feel that I made a huge breakthrough but then wasn't able to follow up the work. Although no official diagnosis had yet been made, I had been told that Mr L seemed to possess quite a few psychopathic tendencies. To dispel some common misconceptions, psychopaths are all around us. In fact many CEO's, surgeons, lawyers and other people apparently at the top of their game possess many psychopathic traits. Most psychopaths have no desire to go around killing people but they are able to function well in certain high stress situations much easier than others, due to their lack of empathy.

As well as a lack of empathy, they often feel little to no fear in situations which would cause panic in the average person. When

For a personal consultation visit: www.themindhealer.co.uk

they do something wrong, they are often aware that it is wrong but it doesn't concern them. Most psychopaths aren't actually violent but if the need arose it wouldn't bother them in the slightest if they had to be and they can often be manipulative.

Mr L was very violent and openly talked about the fact that he enjoys it. He showed a complete lack of remorse when thinking about the people who had been on the receiving end of his violence. He had recently held a knife to his stepfather's throat, threatening to kill him and many suspected it wouldn't be long before he would end up with a long prison sentence.

A great thing about working in schools is that you get to work with people like this who would never normally seek help privately. In fact, when it comes to psychopaths there is nothing to "fix" according to them. Apparently, worried staff had told him that he will literally end up in prison unless he changes his behaviour fast. To this he said that he wouldn't mind that at all and that he would quickly use violence to become top dog in prison.

When he came to see me he was quite glad to get out of lessons and was up for hearing what I had to say. However, he did warn me that whatever I had to say wouldn't make a difference and that he had no desire to change. A quick trawl through his history revealed that he was quite badly bullied at primary school and his parents separated when he was about 12 years old. His mother had been raped recently and she and his step father argued almost constantly.

For a personal consultation visit: www.themindhealer.co.uk

He described some of his violent interactions both in and out of school. He said he got a buzz out of it and wasn't in the least worried that someone might seriously get hurt. When I asked if anything ever bothered him, he said no. I asked if he would feel any upset if his mother died. He said it wouldn't impact him at all although he hopes to exact revenge against the person who raped her.

I encouraged him to adopt a curiosity perspective about our work together rather than dismiss it outright, and asked him to re-live the severe bullying he had endured at primary school. He said at the time it produced very intense anger and now when he thought about it, he felt maybe a little anger but nothing more. He agreed to run a Click Track on it and afterwards said he did feel a little more relaxed but felt relatively calm to start with so not much change.

Even if someone says they feel very relaxed to start with, if it is an unusual case such as this one I will often have them go through the Click Track anyway. This is because they may feel background anger constantly and therefore only realise it was there once it has gone.

The lack of a clear response led me to dig further to see if I could work out a deeper underlying structure and also to see if there were any resources I could gain leverage with. When he was being bullied it became evident that after a long period of it, he felt a rage which led him to attack his bullies, after which the bullying stopped completely. Before that he was rarely angry and was never violent.

For a personal consultation visit: www.themindhealer.co.uk

In terms of the model of reality, it is understandable that it might come to the conclusion that anger and violence lead to safety and respect. Very often anger and other emotions can last for decades after the actual need for it disappears.

The next key event in his life was the separation of his parents. He said he'd prefer they were together but wasn't too fussed. I pressed further and a key important event sprang to his mind from that time. He was very close to his dog and without warning or consultation he was made to give the dog away and he never saw it again. This brought up a definite sense of uneasiness which we cleared with a Click Track.

As with all of my clients, I begin with explaining how the mind works. Now I had this information I presented a potential theory as to he how had gotten to where he was, being prone to violence and not caring about whether he hurt others. I had already explained that anger is a key survival tool and with the apparent success of its use with the bullies, it appears that it got locked in place during the events in primary school.

The next key emotional event was losing his dog without warning. It could be said that his model of reality may have come to the conclusion that it is best not to care for anything or anyone, otherwise you will just end up hurt. His eyes glazed over as I said this and he agreed that this makes sense. This first session was quite a long conversational one and so we had to wait for the next time to pursue this. He seemed quite unfazed when I had presented my possible theory to him. However, apparently straight after he had gone to the head of pastoral support expressing his amazement, saying "I can't believe he figured out about the dog! I haven't thought about the dog for years!". This response was great feedback and evidence that we were on to something. However, despite an increased self-awareness of how things had come about, no further actual changes had been made yet.

In the second session he admitted he was very intrigued by our conversation last time but that he still had no feelings for others and didn't mind if he went to prison. Once I have rapport and respect from someone I can be very direct and they don't take it personally. I suggested that not only was he gaining a sense of safety from attack through using violence but he was also getting his sense of significance through it.

I reminded him that currently his top core value appeared to be significance and this was demonstrated through his lack of concern about going to prison and the fact that his aim would be to be top dog. I suggested that he could maintain his sense of significance just by knowing what he is capable of without actually resorting to any violence.

I also made him aware that there were other ways that he could achieve his sense of significance and that violence is just one method which has many drawbacks. We then went through the advantages and disadvantages of going to prison. Whenever I do this with a client, when it is something to which there is a clear and obvious best answer, I will have us both come up with answers for the side that will benefit them, but I leave it just to them to build up the opposing list. So in this instance we came up with many disadvantages such as losing freedom and many others. The only advantage he could come up with was that he'd still be able to achieve his sense of significance through violence.

Next we discussed other ways in which he could achieve significance. Ones which resonated included starting boxing and exercise in general. We also did pros and cons list of maintaining his current ways of thinking and one of the biggest drawbacks was his lack of a sense of connection with people. It was a double edged sword in that it served to protect him from pain but also made it so he couldn't really enjoy the company of others and so he felt lonely sometimes.

I considered the first session being one in which we drew up a map of the existing model of reality and how it came about. The second session was all about presenting his "guards" with other potential options to fulfil his needs but in ways that had fewer downsides. Without doing this, any potential Click Tracks I suspect would have been met with major resistance in this particular client.

I learned that he began boxing and it had become a key part of his life. Very frustratingly due to school funding, it was a while before I ended up back at that school and by then he had finished. Given more time, the next steps I planned were using PSTEC Negative on beliefs such as, "I have the belief that it is dangerous to have feelings for people", "I have the belief that violence is needed for respect", and those kinds of ideas depending on how our interaction went. This would have been

For a personal consultation visit: www.themindhealer.co.uk

followed up by specific better beliefs and ideas which allowed his needs to remain intact whilst taking a different path in life.

Although I wasn't able to see this case all the way through to the end, it is nice example of a situation in which we really needed to reduce overall resistance before we could use any of the PSTEC tools effectively. Especially in this case, the use of pros and cons and brainstorming with the client to determine whether a change is in their interest was a useful strategy.

It is impossible to say for sure if Mr L really was a psychopath but the label was definitely used by certain staff who had liaised with a clinical psychologist. When a new treatment like PSTEC comes along I think it would be unwise to assume that something which was previously considered untreatable will not respond without proper testing.

Additional Tools

Using the Voice of Respected People

Earlier I talked about the boy who was a fan of Bob Marley and we utilised a lyric in conjunction with PSTEC Positive to make a big change. Another variation of this can be determining if there is a voice of someone a person knows who they respect.

For a personal consultation visit: www.themindhealer.co.uk

For example one lad found it very difficult to behave in school and then became angry the moment he was told off. He said that he behaved well at home because if he did anything wrong his father would say in a stern voice, "you're better than that! Calm down!", or "do you want me to come in there!" When he imagined his father's voice saying this it sent a shiver down his spine because he really respected him and didn't want to disappoint him.

An opportunity like this represents an inner resource within their model of reality. In this instance we identified key times/scenarios which would normally lead to bad behaviour to raise self-awareness and he agreed to imagine his father shouting these sentences which worked to stop the pattern at home. His behaviour substantially improved straight away.

Respected people can include both those known to a client personally, or even famous/public figures. The person also doesn't have to be alive to benefit from their essence as represented in the person's model of reality. By determining such people for a client, they can be asked what advice they would give and then they can imagine that person's voice in their head at key moments.

Internally Re-writing What Others Say

This may sound odd but has proven very effective on multiple occasions. Imagine that there is a key sentence that a loved one or someone else often says to you which really winds you up. This technique involves working out what the hidden message/intent is behind the communication and consciously hearing this as opposed to what they actually say.

For example one lad got caught smoking by his father. It was literally a one off but a month on, every time he was going out his father would say, "you better not be smoking tonight!". The first few times the lad promised his father that he wouldn't do, but as these warnings continued the lad gradually became angrier. I suggested to him that this was his father's way of showing his love for him. The fact that he is worried enough about his wellbeing to be excessive in this manner just shows how much he cares about him. I suggested that the next time it happened for him to rewrite it in his head to, "I love you so please be careful". He grinned at this thought and admitted he had never considered this viewpoint. I also gave him some communication suggestions which would help ease his father's worries. I shall talk more about the specifics of this in a future chapter.

In another similar instance a girl spent half of her time with her mother and the rest with her father. She had a very poor relationship with her mother who was extremely strict and had quite severe curfews for her. This was because the girl regularly smoked marijuana. The girl just saw it as an obstruction to her fun. Obviously her mother was worried about her and with a little digging the girl said that her mother had had big problems with drugs previously in her life.

What is blindingly obvious to external viewers of a scenario can be completely hidden from view from those participating in it. She was shocked at my suggestion that perhaps her mother is simply worried about her making the same mistakes she had made. This one suggestion almost immediately restructured how she was perceiving her mother within her model of reality. She commented that she was experiencing feelings of love for her right there and then that she hadn't felt for some time.

From that point on, if her mother asked her to be in earlier than she would like she heard instead, "I'm worried you will suffer like I did so please come back early". We then used this new perspective as leverage to stop smoking moving forward.

Use of Hand Tapping In the Moment

The PSTEC Click Tracks utilise multiple psychological processes to achieve their amazing success. One of these is classical conditioning, which refers to the fact that when two things happen at once over and over, the brain will form a link between the two. During the Click Tracks certain key words are split second timed to coincide with certain hand tapping. As a result the brain quickly forms a link between the two and can induce feelings of calm just by hand tapping alone.

Once the tracks have been listened to a number of times, many people I have worked with have said that by imagining they are listening to the track in key distressing moments, they often feel

For a personal consultation visit: www.themindhealer.co.uk

much calmer. I believe this will in part be down to classical conditioning and also because if they are in a situation that would normally distress them, our minds have a habit of adding fuel to the fire with negative thinking. By hand tapping and imagining a Click Track, you are utilising brain processes on something neutral/calming, which provides less processing power to be wasted on negative self-talk.

One boy I suggested this method to, instead of discretely tapping on his legs under the table, thought he needed to stand up against the wall and do it there. I have no idea why he thought this would be required but I mentioned this to make it clear that this can be done very discreetly even whilst surrounded by people.

Summary

Here you can see the framework in full flow once more. For many it is a simple case of thinking about the anger trigger and removing with a Click Track. The examples provided show how current anger can often be an after effect of historical traumas. Counterintuitively the trauma is often one that is upsetting so when doing the detective work, don't just be on the lookout for obvious anger triggers.

Like with grief, anxiety and upset, if the cause has occurred very recently, using the standard emotion clearing tracks might be a little less likely to work. On these occasions other approaches

For a personal consultation visit: www.themindhealer.co.uk

might be required, such as belief change, using Cascade Release, general and conceptual reframes, bypassing fear of letting go of anger and so on.

For a personal consultation visit: www.themindhealer.co.uk

Addictions

This chapter will focus on different kinds of addictions but with a strong emphasis on drug addiction. The purpose of this section is to show how widely applicable the general framework is. Although addictions seem completely different to things such as anxiety and anger, there are many commonalities in how I help people with these kinds of problems.

I am not a drug addiction expert so please consult a doctor before making any changes to ensure there won't be dangerous physical side effects. As with most other problems, I ignore the presenting problem initially and hunt out potential historical traumas and current stressors for clearance. There are different causes of addiction but many people use drugs to escape from painful emotions.

Leaving the pain intact whilst trying to cut down or quit a drug still leaves a big problem to be solved. Also, even if the drug is successfully stopped, it stands a greater chance of becoming a problem again, or another "problem" solution may take its place such as overeating.

For a personal consultation visit: www.themindhealer.co.uk

Once the person has cleansed as much as possible and feels relatively calm and happy, only then do we tackle the addiction. Without background and historical stress we have a level playing field. I view the addiction as a combination of a compulsion to do something alongside a habit. In a sense a compulsion is pretty much an emotion; in other words it is a physical feeling in the body that is driving us towards a certain action.

It just so happens that even though on the emotion clearing Click Tracks the wording isn't geared towards removing any particular addictions, it still works very well. As with an emotion I have them rate the desire to do/take something on a scale of 1-10 and note where the sensation is in their body. Next I have then try to maintain that desire whilst going through the Click Track. I encourage them to come to me with a craving so that we have something to work with.

The craving often disappears after one or two listens. I then have them try to bring up the feeling again and in many cases they cannot. If some does come back, simply run the Click Track again. They are often amazed at this change and it is a huge confidence booster. Next we identify potential triggers that will crop up over the coming weeks and come up with a plan of action. The plan of action depends on the individual and what drug they are addicted to.

It always involves coming up with potential stumbling blocks along with a specific set of actions to reduce the risk of relapse. This is done in the spirit of two people - the client and I - solving an external problem. By adopting this perspective it helps to

For a personal consultation visit: www.themindhealer.co.uk

dissociate them from their model of reality and allows questions like, "what tricks might your mind create to drag you back in" to be asked. By being completely open like this it minimises the risk of problems ahead. You will see specific examples of this in some of the case studies you shall now read.

Mr L - childhood abuse and alcoholism

Mr L was about 60 years old and had been an alcoholic for most of his life. With help from his GP and support groups he had managed to reduce his intake to around 4-5 days drinking each week just in the evening. Mentally he was determined to finally quit over the coming weeks.

When he came to see me he hadn't drank for several days and his cravings were quite high. I also had him bring some whiskey which was his drink of choice. A quick scan through his history revealed an incident which occurred when he was 6 years old in which he had been sexually abused. He told me that he had felt "sick" ever since this occurred and that the only thing that ever gave him some relief was drink. He first got drunk when he was 14 and it had been a major part of his life ever since.

Of course this escapism only gave him a brief relief from the bad feeling he was carrying around. One Click Track completely cleared the "sick" feeling which had been present for most of his life. Without clearing this first, any effort to quit may have either been short lived or another problem may have taken its place to mask the old wound.

For a personal consultation visit: www.themindhealer.co.uk

Next I had him sniff the whiskey which sent his already high craving to a 10/10. Two Click Tracks cleared this completely and he looked at the bottle in confusion. He literally had zero urge to drink it, felt he could take it or leave it and was unable to bring back the craving.

Mr L was unusual in that he was already absolutely determined as well as confident he would finally crack this. We began looking for potential triggers and stumbling blocks but he told me this wasn't necessary; in the next few weeks he would simply use the Click Track to help with any cravings that may come up as he thought that that would be the only difficult part. To be clear, he had already checked with his Doctor if it was safe for him to stop completely and indeed it was given the amount he was drinking on the 4 nights he drank. A year previous would have required a slower reduction to begin with.

I saw him a few months later for help with goal setting and confidence and as he had expected, the drink was now a thing of the past. If someone is determined and expecting success, things can go very smoothly. Simply clearing historical trauma and using the Click Tracks to clear cravings were all that were required in this instance. There are different levels of alcoholism and normally much more work would be required. See the next case study for a more typical example of what is required to successfully quit an addictive substance.

Mr S - cocaine heavy use example 1

Mr S used cocaine for many years in social settings. In recent months his use had expanded to using it several times a week and even when alone at home. The increase in usage had coincided with complications towards his ex-wife who was using their daughter as a pawn and turning her against him.

The stress levels about this had reached critical levels and Mr S was really struggling to function day to day. In the first session we cleared a multitude of emotions around his ex-wife and daughter. We also cleared a lot of unresolved grief from several recent bereavements.

He felt quite blissful compared to his usual state of being but at this point we hadn't touched on the cocaine addiction. He said that in the past he had managed to abstain for weeks at a time through willpower but it was incredibly difficult and didn't last. He did this without any physical withdrawal symptoms and because his intake was the same, I wasn't too concerned about any danger on that front.

I advised him to attempt to abstain in the few days leading up to the second session. He managed to do so and took it upon himself to bring along a line of cocaine. His desire/craving was through the roof and he described this as similar to intense sexual excitement.

Two Click Tracks later he was staring dumbfounded at the line of cocaine. He had zero craving or desire to take it at that point

For a personal consultation visit: www.themindhealer.co.uk

in time. He was so amazed that he decided to keep it under his pillow and regularly look at it each day.

He had zero cravings that first night. The following day in the evening the craving came up to a 7/10 but one Click Track cleared it. The ability to control the craving gave him a huge boost of confidence in the process. He used the tracks daily for the first week and in the second week it only came up sporadically.

From that point on the regular cravings disappeared altogether. What remained for a few months were key times at the weekend, certain environments such as particular clubs and pubs as well certain songs which his brain associated with cocaine use.

A few months later even these cravings disappeared. He had several months of no cravings when he went on a city break with friends. His brain still associated drug use with being in an unfamiliar city, on holiday with friends. However, he effortlessly used the track to clear it before it took him over.

Like the previous case, Mr S was absolutely determined which made the process much easier. Contrast this with the next case.

Mr N - cocaine heavy use example 2

Like many people, Mr N began cocaine with recreational use at the weekend which then slowly began to encroach on use during the week. There was a lot of stress at work, which often led to tenseness and arguments at home with his wife. At first glance

For a personal consultation visit: www.themindhealer.co.uk

there didn't appear to be any specific pockets of pain from his past. Clearing the stress about work was a quick and easy matter which left him feeling calm about that area of his life. However, there was still a background sense of unease.

I went back through his timeline and a memory came up from when he was 8 years old. In the memory he had been ridiculed in front of the class by his teacher for struggling to spell a particular word. This put a huge dent in his confidence in school and he pretty much gave up trying after this point and began exhibiting argumentative behaviour. Talking about the memory brought up feelings of "not being good enough". Years later he was diagnosed with dyslexia which explained a lot of things. Thankfully, now schools are much better at identifying and providing help for those pupils with dyslexia.

Because the sense of "not being good enough" had a definite physical manifestation in his stomach, I decided to opt initially for a standard emotion clearing track. This worked fine very quickly and no further belief change work was required. Prior to the session I had requested he abstain for a few days in order to bring up the craving.

The previous emotion clearing work had taken the edge off his craving and it only took one Click Track to clear it completely. I warned him that in the early days, additional use of the Click Tracks might be required to keep the desire at bay. Unlike the person in the previous case, Mr N was less confident in his ability to use the track when feeling the craving come up. We ran out of

For a personal consultation visit: www.themindhealer.co.uk

time and so I suggested we wait and see how things went over the coming few weeks and then troubleshoot if needed.

In the second session he said that he had dramatically reduced his intake but if the craving got higher than 4/10 it always seemed to get the better of him. One key moment was one Friday driving home from work and when he reached a certain road the craving would rise as he would be very close to a dealer's house. He had failed at this point a couple of times in the time between sessions, which then messed up the weekend. Despite this, his use during the week had substantially reduced.

We came up with the following plan. He was to pull over just before he reached that particular road on the way home on Friday. Thinking back he realised that his craving would be just about beginning at this point and he decided exactly where he would pull up so as to leave nothing to chance. Next he would clear the craving with a Click Track and then proceed with the journey.

We also tested out various PSTEC Positive statements and ended up with "I am going to smash this!". As you can see, the sentence on its own doesn't mean much but it did within the context of this situation. His model of reality responded best to this and had him really fired up. During the track he imagined the various problem areas effortlessly being bypassed with our strategy.

He carried out our plan successfully and managed to get past the "problem" road without succumbing. The craving reappeared two hours later when it reached 7pm which is a key Friday trigger

- 263 -

time. Before it reached a 4/10 he ran the Click Track and once again it disappeared. Our brains are all different and compared with the previous case, Mr N's craving disappeared completely after 3 weeks. His main issue was being out of control once 4/10 was reached whereas in the previous example, the ability to override the craving with the Click Track was always present; it was just that the craving was persistent over time.

Mr N had attempted numerous times to quit cocaine previously with different kinds of professional help but nothing had worked. PSTEC was the first time he had something which could clear the craving quickly and reliably. A far as I am aware, it is the only psychological tool which can do such a thing so effectively.

Mr L - marijuana addict who didn't want to quit

Working in schools I often work with children who have an issue which is causing them problems in life but they have no desire to change. In such cases I first build up very strong rapport and help them in other areas. Next I begin baby steps in alleviating the major problem. This is an example of the value and power that great rapport can afford.

I had already helped Mr L with historical domestic violence which had really helped with his anger. However, he was still often agitated even though the intensity had decreased. Like all of his friends he smoked marijuana in the morning before school and then in the evening and he did it to feel calmer and alleviate boredom. He had previously told me he had no desire to change and was pretty determined on the matter.

One day he was particularly agitated and so asked to see me. For some reason he hadn't been able to smoke for two days and it was taking a big toll on him. He was due to pick up some more that evening but didn't think he would make it through the day without getting excluded. By this point I already had good rapport with him and he was familiar with the Click Tracks and one listen removed all of his agitation.

He had no idea that the Click Tracks could have an impact on his cravings and agitation. I reminded him that whenever he goes several days without marijuana he begins to feel so much better and calmer after the initial turmoil. He told me that he couldn't cope with the cravings and also all of his friends smoked and so it would be difficult to cease smoking the weed in their presence.

I said that if I could click my fingers and take away any cravings, boredom and potential friendship issues that might ensue, would he agree that it might benefit him. I asked this question to check if there were any other barriers that needed to be dealt with. He agreed it would benefit him but didn't think he would be capable of resisting. Even if he had the Click Track he said that he thinks he would probably talk himself out of it and he didn't think he'd be able to get to sleep.

I brought in the idea of a series of experiments to test out some changes. I began checking his social situation to see if he had any other non-smoking friends. This was because trying to quit whilst with others who smoke might complicate matters unnecessarily in the early days. He did have another group of friends and felt it might be an option to spend more time with them. I checked for

For a personal consultation visit: www.themindhealer.co.uk

any complications that might arise from this change and he didn't see any.

The other group of friends often played computer games which he enjoyed, so this would help remove the "boredom" barrier. One of his main concerns was struggling to sleep and so for the first week I suggested he allowed himself to smoke half a joint just before bed which he thought would be enough to help him get to sleep.

One big barrier remained. Even though he knew it was massively in his interest to quit, he didn't think he would have the willpower to use the Click Track if a craving came up. He was already aware of the model of reality from our past conversations and was used to talking about his mind with me as though it was something separate from us both.

To further dissociate him from his model of reality I brought up the idea of "parts". In other words a logical, adult part of him knew that the best thing long term would be to quit, yet another part wanted the immediate gratification and didn't want to change. I asked what he thought it might require to prevent the other part from sabotaging the process. He said that if his mother didn't give him any money, he wouldn't be able to buy any and so it would be out of his hands.

I asked permission for the school to contact his mother to discuss our conversation and to ask that she doesn't give him any money for the next month. The deep rapport with me and dissociation with his model of reality led him to agree to this, whilst at the same time the other part of him was saying, "I can't believe I am agreeing to this!"

He had enough left to last the following week just before bed and so sleep wouldn't be an issue, at least initially. With the lack of money, new friends/activities to do and the Click Tracks to help deal with cravings and sleep, the results were quick and easy. Over that month he appeared physically different; much brighter and his agitation disappeared and he was able to get on with work much easier.

In this case we identified potential resources to employ in the form of changing friends and new activities. We also identified negative resources which in this case turned out to be money from parents which was fuelling the problem and used rapport and dissociation to cut that off at the stem.

Summary

I have less experience helping those with addictions compared with other problems. However, I thought it might be useful to demonstrate how addictions can be worked on within the framework already outlined. In particular, viewing the cravings/desire simply as an emotion to be cleared.

I just want to reiterate that I am not an expert in this field and it is essential you seek medical approval before embarking on any change to drug use for yourself or a client.

For a personal consultation visit: www.themindhealer.co.uk

Interpersonal Skills and Conflict Resolution

This is an area that I find fascinating. Often by using just slightly different words along with a different inner script, radically different responses can result. Within the general framework this is one of the "outer" sections which can be used as a piece of action to be carried out to improve a situation once the initial clearing has occurred.

It makes good use of some of the ideas discussed in the early sections of this book in terms of bypassing a person's guards to impact their model of reality. I talked about similar ideas in PSTEC Advanced Part 2 but here are examples which don't involve having to do much background work with characters and so are slicker and less time consuming. This is only skimming the surface here but some important ideas will be discussed and importantly, it will further expand upon the idea of our brain having guards, but this time crucially how to get past those guards to instigate change.

For a personal consultation visit: www.themindhealer.co.uk

Inner Script

Before I began work as a therapist, I was of the opinion that we pretty much all had free will. One consequence of believing this philosophical maxim is that you assume that other people's actions are all consciously intended. This, in turn, naturally leads to the belief that, when others hurt us, it is intentional. This belief quickly unravelled as I began to see how many blind spots we all have, how hidden influences play a role through our emotions and how we don't choose how all of this fits together. Rather, random life occurrences play a huge role in how our emotional and thought levers are positioned; in other words how our model of reality is configured.

A quick introspection can remind us that there will have been many occasions when we have felt anger or upset for example, yet we didn't choose to feel these things in the moment. Rather they occurred automatically and in a sense greatly reduce our capacity to act on our own free will in that moment. Moreover, those strong feelings can have a dramatic impact on our behaviour. Really grasping this allows a person to analyse a situation in a detached manner and become outcome focused rather than reactive.

Another "feature" of our minds is that many of us assume that others are interpreting a situation from our viewpoint. In fact many people don't see their interpretation as just a viewpoint but rather as actual reality itself. By now I hope it is becoming clear that we each have our own unique narrative as to what is

For a personal consultation visit: www.themindhealer.co.uk

occurring and there are an infinite number of ways of interpreting any specific event. This hidden assumption causes people to "negative mind read"; this means that we assume that others know our intentions and thoughts. After all if we believe that others see the world as we do, then something that seems obvious to us, we mistakenly believe should be obvious to others too.

If we want to instigate a different outcome in another person, then we need to change their model of reality. To do this we need to pass information into their minds without it first being intercepted by their "guards". In other words we need to present the information in such a way that it isn't interpreted as some kind of attack. If a perceived attack occurs, whether it has occurred in actuality or not, the other person's guards become activated and no change will be made.

All this will sound quite abstract so here are some case studies which will show these ideas in action.

Mr L - severe arguing between mother and sister

Mr L was very tired and stressed. For the past 18 months his mother and sister had been arguing every single night until the early hours of the morning which meant that he didn't get much sleep. As a result, home life was unpleasant and it was impacting his experience in school.

He told me that he had repeatedly asked them to stop arguing but it didn't seem to make a difference. So how could we

For a personal consultation visit: www.themindhealer.co.uk

possibly make a difference when the problem seemed to be quite a large one involving people who I would never see? First we came up with a preferred outcome which was that he was exposed to as little arguing as possible and that it ended earlier to avoid it impacting his sleep.

As I expected, every time he had asked them to stop arguing up until now was whilst they were mid-argument. In other words when both of their guards were on high alert and therefore any information/request that was presented at that time would very likely be rejected without any proper consideration.

I suggested he has a conversation with his mother when his sister wasn't there. In that conversation he was to say that he knew that his mother and sister weren't choosing to argue on purpose. However, he was to explain that he is struggling to sleep because of it and feeling stressed a result. Next he would ask if it would be ok if they went outside and argued in the car so that he didn't have to listen to it all.

Although this request sounds quite bizarre, its sole aim was to pass on information about the detrimental impact that their behaviour was having on him without her guards being activated. Rather than ask them to stop arguing, he just asked if they could change the location of where they argued. This was to minimize the chance that she would respond confrontationally. I didn't know much about her and so wanted to bypass all potential resistance.

For a personal consultation visit: www.themindhealer.co.uk

He was very sceptical that this would have any impact but agreed to try it as an experiment. I saw him a week later and he looked transformed. Since this conversation, his mother and sister hadn't argued once. Once the information had been processed without resistance, in effect it popped the reality tunnel that mother and sister had found themselves in. Once patterns emerge like this they can become rigid, habitual and trancelike. However, so long as there isn't a deeper underlying issue, even interactions which seem completely locked in place can de-escalate very quickly. This kind of result, using these insights occur many times a week for my clients.

Miss H - lack of attention from mother and bullying advice

Miss H was feeling down. One of the things bothering her was that she felt that her relationship with mother wasn't great and that her mother didn't seem to show much interest in her. A key aspect of this was that when her mother picked her up, Miss H would ask her mother about her day but this was never reciprocated. She then would conclude that her mother wasn't interested in her and so kept her distance for the rest of the night.

I explained to Miss H that we each have different blind spots. What we might consider simple good manners, for someone else might be completely off the radar. I suggested that either through stress or some other reason, it just might not be occurring to her mother at this point in time to ask how her day had gone. This is a completely different scenario to one in which her mother considers asking about her day but can't be bothered.

For a personal consultation visit: www.themindhealer.co.uk

We agreed that the outcome she was after was a little more attention and interest to be shown to her by her mother, especially when she was being picked up from school. In order to be met with the least amount of resistance, this information had to be presented to her mother, whilst aiming to bypass any defence mechanisms. Typically, a person may feel a build-up of hurt and resentment over time and when the information finally gets transmitted, the other person's defence mechanisms will be activated due to the perceived attack, thus making change less likely.

I suggested that we assume that it is simply a current blind spot of her mother's to begin with. With this in mind, after asking her mother how her day had gone, she was to simply ask if she would start asking how her day had gone. The attitude in which it was said was very important; it was to be said with the attitude that she was asking for a simple favour without any hint of hurt or accusation.

Miss H took some convincing to try this but she took a leap of faith and tried it that afternoon. Apparently, her mother laughed and asked her how her day had gone. From that point forward her mother asked her everyday how her day had gone and their relationship greatly improved. Often just one small change such as this can act as a catalyst for much greater change. I suspect that up until this point, Miss H was harbouring resentment over this and therefore may have withdrawn from her mother for the rest of the night as a result. Therefore once this change was instigated, other aspects of their relationship had a chance to flourish such as spending more time together in the evenings.

For a personal consultation visit: www.themindhealer.co.uk

Miss H was also experiencing some friendship issues. Recently one of the girls in her group had begun being very confrontational, controlling and intimidating to Miss H and her friends. Miss H felt scared of her although physically, she felt confident that if it came to a fight she would do well, so the fear wasn't one of physical violence. She told me that the other girls also appeared unsettled by her behaviour but thought that if she plucked up the courage to confront her, the other girls may stick up for the troubled girl as Miss H was a relative newcomer to the group.

It was a very complex and strange dynamic. The solution is a very useful lesson on the topic of confrontation, which is something that makes many people feel anxious. It also shows how quickly an entire group dynamic can be changed when communicating information in a way that bypasses the guards of certain key people.

Step one involved checking in with the other people of the group to get their thoughts whilst minimizing any friction this could cause. This involved speaking to each individual in the group alone and rather than complain/call the girl in question, she was to express concern that she doesn't seem to be herself recently. Miss H wasn't aware of anything that had gone on but I suggested that maybe something was bothering the problem girl, which in turn was impacting her behaviour. She was also going to get their thoughts on whether she should check in with the girl to see if everything was alright. She had a fear that as a relative newcomer to the group, they may reject her if she rocks the boat so this last step was to alleviate this fear.

The "problem" girl's behaviour had been quite appalling but rather than make any accusations, she was to take her to one side and ask her if everything was ok because "she hadn't seemed herself recently". Miss H carried out these instructions and when she asked the problem girl if everything was ok, she immediately began crying and opened up that it is looking like her parents might be separating and that she is really struggling to deal with it. This one act of showing concern popped the girl's "reality tunnel" and with her fears brought out into the open, her behaviour changed quickly.

When people are experiencing a lot of negative emotions, they can often say or do things which they would never otherwise consider. If Miss H had told the girl that she was out of order for her behaviour, defences would have been raised and a fight likely would have ensued, given Miss H's description of how she had been.

In this way many confrontations can be completely sidestepped. When Miss H asked her mother if she would mind asking how her day had gone, it was a simple blind spot which was made visible. If there was a deeper underlying reason for the apparent absence of interest shown, then useful information would likely have been revealed by her mother, which could then be tackled directly.

Similarly, by expressing concern at her friend's behaviour rather than anger, what would have likely resulted in a violent confrontation was bypassed and the outcome of behaviour modification was achieved. If the girl had said that nothing had

For a personal consultation visit: www.themindhealer.co.uk

been wrong, then perhaps other ideas and/or boundaries would need to have been decided upon and carried out. In my experience so many problems simply disappear by communicating within the guidelines of this framework.

Mr C - bullied for being slightly deaf

Mr C had to wear a hearing aid and the other kids often made fun and bullied him about this. This happened on the bus on his way home more than any other time and the thought of it made him very angry. One metaphor I often use in a situation like this is that currently, when they make fun of him, it is like they are prodding a wound and as a result it is creating a lot of emotional pain. However if we healed this wound, when they made fun of him it might still be annoying but that it is more like a fly landing on you; in other words you'd rather it not happen but it isn't a big deal.

I then had him picture the problem scenario and build up the anger which we then cleared with a Click Track. Afterwards he wasn't able to build up any anger at the thought of it. We then chatted about what exactly happens and I said it is likely that he will be less bothered now if they say anything which will actually reduce the risk of it happening in the future. He disputed this and said that he has already told them that it doesn't bother him, but he admitted that he said this in a state of agitation which indirectly communicates the opposite.

I explained that now, emotionally, he really wasn't that bothered which would alter the dynamics involved. I also suggested an

For a personal consultation visit: www.themindhealer.co.uk

experiment; the next time they tried to wind him up he would pretend not to hear them and ask them to repeat over and over until they got bored of asking. Doing this from a place of calm, in effect turns the tables. It shows that he really isn't bothered as well as putting him in a position of toying with them. He tried this and literally the bullying stopped overnight. I suggested that even if it did carry on that it wasn't such a big deal now he felt calmer about the whole situation following the Click Track

This pattern is so common and reliable. The bullies/problem people are hoping to get some kind of emotional response from the target as it makes them feel significant. As soon as the emotional response disappears, then the intended purpose is no longer satisfied and they therefore have no good reason to continue.

Miss K - transgender person being bullied

I had already worked with Miss K to clear social anxiety and other emotional ailments and she was in a relatively good place. However, one problem still remained; two people in one of her classes asked her questions about the process she was going through. She didn't mind answering the questions but they asked her the same questions every day and she felt that they might be making fun of her.

She felt anxious about potentially confronting them about it. We cleared the anxiety with a Click Track and then came up with some communication ideas about how to tackle it. Rather than do it from a position of attack I explained we would be better of conveying the information and her desire for them to stop questioning her whilst bypassing their "guards".

She admitted that although it is annoying, it could just be that because it is such an unfamiliar topic for many people, they may just be genuinely curious. By assuming this she agreed to say something along the lines of, "I know you're interested but is it ok if we stop talking about it now as I'm getting a bit fed up with talking about it all of the time". This statement doesn't make anyone "wrong" and at the same time conveys the request for them to stop. She was instructed to say this from a place of simply requesting a favour rather than frustration.

If they stopped asking the questions following this request, then we have achieved the desired outcome and it will suggest that they were just genuinely interested. She was a little worried what to do if it continued and so we came up with follow up steps. She was to remind them one more time but if they carried on after that, their intent was definitely to cause her distress.

At that point she would suggest in a calm manner that if they continue asking questions she would have to speak to the head of year to complain. This is an example of setting boundaries in a calm manner and explaining what will happen if the problem continues. Communicating in this way reduces the risk of anger being generated which in turn makes the chance of information getting through without being batted away more likely. She followed these instructions and the questions stopped right after the initial request.

For a personal consultation visit: www.themindhealer.co.uk

Miss L - reframing relationships

Since her parents had separated, Miss L still spoke to her father but for some reason unknown to her, her grandparents and the rest of that side of her family had rejected her completely, which was a big shock as she had always been close to them. Obviously, for some reason they must have been hurt by the break up but it was quite a strange situation.

Many months had passed and it transpired that she was about to visit her grandparents for the first time at the weekend. She had a mix of feelings ranging from anger, anxiety at the thought she might get rejected again as well as a little excitement that things might get back to normal again.

She mostly shifted from panic to anger though and agreed that it would be best if we could turn these unhelpful feelings down. A Click Track left her feeling much more relaxed so I then set about giving her some useful frames through which to view the situation. I reminded her that, to a large extent, we are all a victim of our emotions which play a big role in how we think and behave. She had first-hand experience in this just now as she wasn't choosing to feel the emotions she was feeling.

I suggested that maybe they felt really hurt and disappointed at the break up and that maybe it was too painful to see her as it reminded them of what had happened. I made it clear that this was no excuse but that strong feelings make people do things they would never do under normal circumstances.

For a personal consultation visit: www.themindhealer.co.uk

Next I sought out resources in her own life. She was a very popular girl with many friends and was confident and happy in general. I pointed out that even though she hadn't seen her grandparents for a long while, most of the time she was just fine. All this was presented with the aim of relegating the desire to have a relationship with her grandparents from a need to a preference.

The next frame I utilised was that of this being a test to see how things had changed. In the very unlikely event she would be rejected again (unlikely because they probably wouldn't have agreed to see her otherwise), does she really need people in her life who hold grudges against someone who has done no wrong? I said that if they do still hold some kind of a grudge, it will likely be caused by emotions beyond their control, which over time may dissipate. At that point they may be more open to getting the relationship back to how it used to be but that would be up to Miss L to decide if she wanted this.

The purpose of the entire conversation was to engender the expectation of success whilst massively reducing any potential damage that could have been caused if they had acted with malice of any kind. We ran a PSTEC Positive on, "whatever happens on Saturday, everything is still going to be ok". She added the word "still" in to ramp up the truth that she is already doing just fine.
She went along feeling calm and confident and her grandparents were very apologetic. They resumed their relationship and everything was fine.

For a personal consultation visit: www.themindhealer.co.uk

Using an Unexpected Conversation/Action to Instigate Change

You will have already seen this in the examples above but once negative emotions have been cleared towards a person for whom a better relationship would be in everyone's best interest, initiating a conversation they wouldn't expect can make a huge impact and kick start change.

In the example of school children who have developed a bad relationship dynamic with a teacher, first of all I clear the emotion. Next I suggest reasons why the teacher might be thinking/feeling/behaving in the way they are and then explain how dynamics can easily go down a bad path without anyone really being to blame.

Next I suggest that they approach the teacher outside of class time. It's difficult to give specifics about what exactly to say as it will differ from situation to situation. However imagine this scenario; a boy gets bored after 10 minutes in a particular class and so starts talking or messing about with his mates. The teacher obviously needs to teach and so the boy gets in trouble. The boy often gets angry when being told off regardless of the cause and the battle ensues. From this point on the teacher will often blame the boy for things, when it isn't obvious who is the culprit, just because she expects him to be involved.

I see this exact situation several times a day. Once we have cleared the emotion and given him some useful frames through which to view the situation, we come up with a practical solution for the boredom problem. For example one boy might feel that if he has a stress ball, the minute he starts feeling bored/agitated, he could start toying with that rather than going through his usual behaviour patterns and getting in trouble. In fact this one action could change everything.

Next I suggest that the child has a conversation with the teacher. When he approaches the teacher he could say that he has been speaking to me and realised how difficult he has been making her life. Next he would tell her what he is going to start doing when he feels agitated instead of disrupting the class. He then asks if they could have a fresh start. For a teacher, to have a childish and unruly boy come to you to ask for a fresh start, is very unexpected and can create confusion. Confusion is a very good state for anyone to be in to absorb information from someone else; it means pre-existing patterns aren't in play which allows new ways of being to come into play. The boy might then say that he understands why he often gets in trouble but asks if she would start giving him the benefit of the doubt from now on? You would not believe how often I carry out this kind of process/instruction and it works magically.

In another scenario imagine a child who has a poor relationship with a parent. Normally certain conflicts may have arisen at some point which escalated into constant background anger and then spending as little time as possible with each other. This is another very common scenario.

For a personal consultation visit: www.themindhealer.co.uk

As above we begin by clearing as much background anger as possible and explain how this type of conflict develops and grows out of control. We also analyse key trigger points and come up with solutions for those. For example if one child is asked to tidy their room but only does it hours later which causes an argument, they would then just do it at the moment they are asked. It is easy to analyse problem patterns and come up with better patterns from a place of calm. Next, I check if they have ever had a good relationship at some point with the parent and most people have. They often say they would like it to get back to how it was but can't see how that would happen.

I explain that once we change the emotions of one person in a dynamic, the entire dynamic can change quickly and easily. I say that now their anger towards the parent has gone, many arguments simply won't happen because pre-existing triggers won't have the same impact. Once they confirm they would like a better relationship with the other person we come up with a plan.

First we figure out specific activities that the two of them could both do which they would both enjoy. We brainstorm this and seek out the ones which would have the least chance of being rejected for reasons such as being too expensive. Once we have a few options they are to have a chat with the parent and ask if they could have some quality time together and get things back to how they used to be.

Because the child is much calmer, the parent will sense this. Equally important, the parent will likely be shocked as this

For a personal consultation visit: www.themindhealer.co.uk

request is probably very unexpected. Unless the problem is very severe and there is obvious neglect involved, most of the time this one conversation transforms the relationship. When I first began creating these kinds of tasks, I assumed that much more work would be required moving forward but to my pleasant surprise, this combination of processes, frames and tasks seems to provide such a jolt that both parties are keen to maintain the new status quo.

Summary

These cases are focused on children but the principles remain the same in any human interaction. First realise that we are all victims of our own life experiences which, to a huge extent, dictate our feelings, thoughts and behaviours. This is easily done by looking inwardly and observing times when your actions have been governed by how you felt at a certain time.

Next, realise that unless someone is really damaged (which again is no fault of their own), most of us just want to get on with people and not hurt them. Most of the time a problem dynamic is just two people doing the best that they can but are stuck in a pattern trap.

Once these ideas have been digested it becomes obvious that we need to figure out what outcome we are after and to start figuring out the easiest way to achieve this outcome with someone. The outcome may be a better relationship with

For a personal consultation visit: www.themindhealer.co.uk

someone, or having another person modify their behaviour in some way.

Next, the person who wants to instigate change should clear as much emotion linked to the other person as possible so that they can see with clarity and also to remove as many problem triggers as possible. It is helpful at this point to see how they could modify their own behaviour to increase the chance of success.

Once all of this has been done, a conversation is a good next step. The conversation is designed to bypass the other person's guards to increase the chance the information will be processed properly. This means do not bring any blame or anger to the situation as this will do the opposite. Prior to the conversation it is a good idea to think of particular perspectives which make you feel ok whether the outcome being reached or not, as with the girl who feared rejection from her grandparents.

If the desired outcome isn't reached, the next step is to lay out boundaries from a place of calm. For example the transgender girl who was being questioned daily said that if XYZ happened again she would regretfully have to speak to the head of year. Another person might say he really wants to visit the other person but he finds certain behaviours they are doing distressing and so he will have to visit less or not at all.

This chapter deserves to be a full book in its own right but hopefully you will find some of these ways of thinking about relationship dynamics of interest and use. The ideas should also

For a personal consultation visit: www.themindhealer.co.uk

show the entire framework from a different viewpoint, thus making the overall picture clearer.

Autism Spectrum Disorder (ASD), Tourette's, Attention Deficit Hyperactivity Disorder (ADHD)

This chapter groups together a number of issues which you may come across or may suffer from along with some practical advice and things to take into account. There isn't much difference to the usual order of proceedings I go through in terms of the framework. However, there is often an emphasis on different sections, and the work may be more ongoing in nature. I am certainly not an expert in these areas but I have been pleasantly surprised by the results obtained using the ideas in this book.

ASD

Most of the people with ASD I have worked with have responded to PSTEC extremely well. A lot of it depends on where they are on the Spectrum. Those who are more severely autistic are less likely to respond compared with those who present milder forms of the condition. They tend to become angrier or anxious more easily and typically need to use the tracks more systematically. They are also more likely than others to benefit from the relationship dynamic information already discussed in the last chapter, to give them a framework through which to view relationships. I shall begin with a couple of people who were too severely autistic to benefit.

Mr L - lack of desire to change

Mr L had a lot of anger towards certain people who had been teasing him about his hair. He had no intention of altering his hairstyle and when I asked if his anger so far had stopped them from teasing him, he replied that it hadn't. I told him about PSTEC and how it could switch off his anger response in this situation. Also, I explained that by doing so the teasing would very likely stop as all those people really wanted was the emotional response he was giving him.

Mr L thought it a very odd idea that getting rid of the anger might help and wouldn't even contemplate the notion. Rigidity of thinking can be a feature of those with ASD and in this instance it provided enough of a barrier that he didn't want to try out new approaches to alleviate the stress from the situation. This is by no means a typical response though and so it will depend on each individual person and how their ASD manifests.

Mr T - depression

Mr T was in a very low mood and had been for some time. School had asked me to see him as he was very bright but he seemed to be making no effort in the important build up to his summer exams. His parents had separated the year before and there was a rough correlation between this and his feelings of depression. Previous to this, other than the difficulties that people with ASD sometimes experience, he was generally calm and happy.

To ease him into the process we ran a Click Track on the upset he felt about his parent's divorce. The Click Track revealed a belief that happiness and feelings are just a hindrance to his goals. When we scrutinised this, a Pandora's Box of beliefs and thoughts sprang forth.

When his parents were going through the rough time, Mr T felt a lot of anger. There was an incident with his friends at around this time in which he got very angry and he felt he took it out on them. Since then, he rejected his friends and they had no idea why; in his mind he was protecting them.

Throughout all of this he came to the conclusion that all emotions, whether good or bad are a hindrance to his goals. He therefore stopped doing anything that made him happy, such as seeing friends and doing fun things. He also claimed he was able to detach himself from any bad feelings, though it was clear he was very low.

His school became a little concerned because at around this time he also stopped doing any work, whereas previously he was very industrious. He says he felt like a failure and this belief was removing any motivation he had to do any work. Mr T had frequently used the word goal and goals so I suspected that concept was a key one and so decided to pursue that aspect of his model of reality.

His overarching goal was to change the world by creating a machine which could alter the structure of atoms. He says he has a committee in his head for this project alone and his lack of progress on this goal had led to some of the members of the committee conclude that he must be a failure. Also, they said that he wasn't worth anything without the accomplishment of this goal. These ideas of failure obviously aren't a great reality tunnel through which to get lots of academic work done.

To check for other potential subconscious resistance I had him say out loud, "It is safe to feel better". The belief that, "If I get better I am gone" then revealed itself, meaning that he felt he needed this inner turmoil there to have any chance of accomplishing his goal and that his identity is based on this accomplishment. Moreover, he needed to redeem himself by saving the world.

Before challenging a particular belief, I always try to get the full picture as all knowledge within a model of reality is part of a bigger matrix. By this point he agreed that holding himself to such lofty goals combined with a judgement of failure if he doesn't meet them, actually makes success far less likely. I reminded him that it is stopping him at the first hurdle of secondary (high) school education.

We analysed each of the beliefs from other perspectives to weaken their rigidity and discussed other people who had accomplished great things and how for most of them it wasn't

For a personal consultation visit: www.themindhealer.co.uk

plain sailing. At the time of this session PSTEC Negative hadn't been created but he could feel subconscious resistance to feeling better, linked with the belief he mentioned earlier about emotions greatly reducing any chance of success.

Because there was a definite feeling attached to the subconscious resistance, I ran a standard Click Track on it whilst he was thinking about those ideas and this cleared it (a Cascade Release could have been used here too if needed) and he felt quite a bit calmer than he had done for a while. As the track was playing, a readymade PSTEC Positive statement had begun forming in his mind of "everything is enjoyable".

When the subconscious mind serves a statement up like this, so long as it feels good when saying it out loud, it is perhaps a good idea to run it through PSTEC Positive. He was buzzing and felt good for the first time in a long time. In later weeks he reignited his friendships and saw his school work as just a stepping stone. This perspective helped him get back on track and not suffer the enormity of the burden of thinking that he had the weight of the world on his shoulders.

More ongoing work was required in different areas but this was a key breakthrough for Mr T. As can be seen here, sometimes those with ASD might have less common thought patterns and beliefs but they can often be worked on in the same way.

For a personal consultation visit: www.themindhealer.co.uk

Mr B - trigger words

Mr B had no idea why but certain trigger words produced a severe anxiety response in him. In fact just the thought that someone might say one of them was enough to send him into panic. We are all capable of having trigger words but for those with ASD, the response can be more severe than it might otherwise be.

Saying the words out loud would have been too overwhelming for Mr B but when I suggested that he imagined one of the words spray painted in a wall in small letters, he felt that this would bring up a more manageable amount of anxiety to work with. Because his anxiety was prone to going very high very quickly, I had him practice a few minutes of a Click Track in a calm state so he wasn't in a position of having to learn something new in a position of very high anxiety, if it happened to head in that direction.

We started with one trigger word but almost immediately after starting the Click Track he began yawning. At the end he said that he had added the other trigger words on the wall and none of them bothered him any more.

Miss J - anger towards people

People with ASD often have more intense feelings in general. Miss J had severe anger towards a small number of girls who regularly tried to wind her up. Before this she wasn't an angry person but since then she often snapped at people.

For a personal consultation visit: www.themindhealer.co.uk

There appeared to be nothing historically playing a role. She shook with rage at the thought of these girls and a Click Track completely cleared this. She was mature and took on-board many of the reframes I suggested. However, even with the clearing, each time the girls teased her, anger would result. However she now had a routine to follow; she would take herself out of the situation and listen to a Click Track which calmed her down within minutes and allowed her to enjoy the rest of her day.

Had I more time to work with her in the realm of beliefs and reframes, we could potentially have made more of a lasting impact. However as a general rule of thumb, I have found that those with ASD are more likely to have to use techniques and strategies more systematically than other people might have to. Even though regular use may be required, it can still dramatically improve their day to day experience.

Tourette's Syndrome

My experience with Tourette's is limited but I thought it prudent to include my experiences so far here. As in all cases whatever the issue I begin clearing as much life trauma as possible as the cause of so many presenting symptoms are locked within past events.

Tics often have a habit of increasing in intensity and frequency when the person is stressed or suffering in some other way emotionally. One girl I worked with had severe exam anxiety and her tics were very pronounced but by the end of the Click Track her tics had literally stopped completely at that point in time due to the removal of stress. This scenario has happened repeatedly in my experience.

For various reasons other than the initial session and experiencing the Click Track, I have never had the chance to delve deeper to see if the PSTEC Suite of tools could help alleviate the symptoms even more. I am aware that those I have helped have greatly benefited from the ongoing use of Click Tracks and because they are more relaxed, tend to suffer less with tics and other symptoms.

One person had particular social anxiety when being served in a shop and as a result his tics grew much worse in that environment. Anxiety at the thought of being served came up which we removed with a Click Track. We then did some simple belief change work and used PSTEC Positive to engender the expectation that he would feel calm and confident the next time he was in a shop. This had a huge impact whenever he was in a shop from that point on. An occasional tic might occur but he actually felt even calmer than normal in a shop situation than in other neutral situations, after this work.

It would be great to see how much this approach could alleviate the symptoms of those suffering from Tourette's. I suspect much of the benefit would come indirectly through helping the person feel much calmer. It would also be great to see whether a Tourette's sufferer who had become familiar with the Click

Tracks, could then imagine the Click Track process if ever their tics became more pronounced and whether this would help.

Attention Deficit Hyperactivity Disorder (ADHD)

ADHD is a group of behavioural symptoms that include inattentiveness, hyperactivity and impulsiveness. The cause is unknown and there is evidence that the brains of those suffering with ADHD are different to those who do not.

I do not believe that techniques such as PSTEC can cure this disorder but it can have a profound impact in my experience, especially in helping the person to feel calmer in the moment. I have worked with many children who suffer from severe ADHD and even when they are bouncing off the walls having forgotten to take their medication, often just one round of a Click Track without thinking about anything in particular, leaves them feeling very calm. In my experience this happens very quickly.

However it isn't a one off fix and they would need to use it as and when needed but it is a great little tool they can use to take some control over their symptoms when it gets too much.

For a personal consultation visit: www.themindhealer.co.uk

Cascade Release Tips and Tricks

Cascade Release is probably one of the lesser used tools within the PSTEC Suite of Tools. The other tools are so powerful that often there isn't a great need for it. However, occasionally it is the perfect tool for the job. For those unfamiliar with it here is a quick intro.

Cascade Release is primarily used for when there is a feeling that you or your clients aren't sure of the cause. In those scenarios you can sometimes just guess what the problem is, or even create a fictitious scenario which includes what seem to be relevant themes and then aim a Click Track at that scene in the mind. For example, if someone feels anxious and trapped, they could imagine that they are trapped somewhere and focus on that whilst going through a Click Track.

All of our brains and models of reality are different and so it is good to have multiples ways to achieve the same goal. I have worked with some people for whom Cascade Release has been the only thing that has made an impact (though this isn't the case of most of the time).

For a personal consultation visit: www.themindhealer.co.uk

It works differently than the rest of the tracks in that your subconscious mind is instructed to perform a task out of your awareness. The task that your subconscious mind is given is to identify anything related to the current bad feeling and to push it into the future so it hasn't happened yet. In phase two the task is repeated but this time the subconscious mind is told to remove the unhelpful thoughts and feelings from floating about in the future and to put them into the "trash can" of the mind.

Throughout this, the person has their hand held up like a lever and their subconscious mind is instructed to slowly lower it to their lap as the work is carried out, to indicate progress. The process should take about 4-5 minutes for each of the two phases. With the other hand they are to tap along whenever they hear the Clicks which occasionally speed up and slow down.

When working with clients I often give them a visual demonstration so they have some idea as to the speed of descent that their arm should take. I have found that some people have their arm held up for a while without much pain or discomfort whilst others really struggle; surprisingly it is sometimes those with more athletic arms who struggle. If they are struggling I tell them to balance their elbow on the arm of the chair (or whatever they are sat on) and lower it from there. When they do this they can sometimes have a tendency to take too long to lower their hand so I give another visual demonstration of how fast it should go down.

The subconscious mind should be in charge with monitoring how much work has been done and so should be in charge of the

For a personal consultation visit: www.themindhealer.co.uk

speed of descent. However, a reminder every so often (to remember to allow the arm to lower) can make things smoother for some people. With clients when it nears the end of the audio track, if their arm still has a little way to go I will quickly rewind the track back to an earlier section. This happens so quickly they are often unaware that anything has happened and I also warn them that if they hear a slight pause in the recording to just carry on as they were. If they are going so slow that their arm is nowhere near touching their lap, earlier in the process I will have already reminded them to allow their arm to slowly fall.

To reduce the risk of any subconscious resistance I will explain beforehand that no memories will or can be deleted. Rather it is the damaging qualities of the experience which will be made redundant. I also suggest that the subconscious mind will always keep hold of any valuable information from whatever is worked on.

Cascade Release is great for those who, for whatever reason, struggle with the tapping process. I have already mentioned in different sections that it can be a useful tool to try when removing anger, if the normal Click Tracks inadvertently increase the anger, for whatever reason. This is often because a part of them thinks that doing so might result in danger.

As time has progressed I am more likely to go down the belief change path as a first port of call rather than Cascade Release for situations like this in which anger increases. For example this may involve having them say out loud, "It is safe to feel calm" or "It is safe to let go of this anger" to check for any subconscious

For a personal consultation visit: www.themindhealer.co.uk

resistance which would come in the form of an emotion or an outright refusal of the client to say it. If this is the case it can be more practical to analyse the situation with the client to see if we can mutually find better ways of looking at it which allow them to feel safe even without the anger.

Miss K - cascade release and mental landscape

Miss K had been through a lot and had been in great emotional pain for decades. In describing how she felt, she often gave very vivid visual descriptions of what she was experiencing. We did a lot of work but a particular breakthrough occurred whilst using Cascade Release.

She had begun spontaneously describing her situation as being like standing in the middle of a burnt out field. Half way across the field was a giant intimidating wall, about 100 foot tall made out of big black bricks. Whilst stood on this field the key emotion she felt was despair.

Whenever anyone describes a fully formed metaphor like this, I will often dive in and see if making changes to it in their imagination alters how they are feeling. This is an extremely powerful methodology and often just asking them to change the attributes of the key elements involved such as colour, size, shape and location can produce dramatic changes in how they feel.

In this instance I asked her to describe the scene vividly. The subconscious mind works in symbols and I suspect that on the other side of this wall lay more pleasant emotional pastures. I had

For a personal consultation visit: www.themindhealer.co.uk

her walk up to the wall and imagine a ladder materialising that goes right to the top. She did this and I had her climb to the top to see what was on the other side. She attempted this but the higher she climbed, the higher the wall grew. I asked her to halt the growth of the wall and climb to the top.

Often you can be quite authoritarian within these mental landscapes and some of the time the subconscious obeys you. This wasn't one of those occasions so I had her climb back down the wall. At this point PSTEC Negative hadn't been released and I hadn't yet dreamed up the method of saying certain statements out loud to determine the specific nature of subconscious resistance. However, this is a clear manifestation of subconscious resistance in visual format.

I therefore asked her to imagine that she had a little hammer and chisel. I then told her that we are going to stay on this side of the wall but use the hammer and chisel to create a little hole in the wall just so we could see what was on the other side. I made it clear we were staying on this side of the wall to reduce the risk that the subconscious mind may sabotage this action.

She was able to create the hole and on the other side was a beautiful landscape of bright green fields, flowers, animals and the overarching feeling she got from that place was a sense of deep inner peace. However to get there we needed to get over the wall.

We had already cleared a huge amount of historical trauma but either there was something we had missed, or this symbology was

For a personal consultation visit: www.themindhealer.co.uk

purely a visual representation of the belief that she would be in danger if she felt safe and at peace.

I decided to use the Cascade Release but rather than just focus on the feeling, I had her imagine this landscape throughout the tracks. Throughout the process her body began making all sorts of noises inside like air pockets rumbling and moving about. Although this kind of response isn't typical, it is normal and can be expected occasionally with the release of negative emotions.

The impact on her was profound. She described how during the track, within her mental landscape a tornado had slowly moved in from the distance and as it got nearer the wall, bits of brick began flying off into the sky and disappearing. By the end of the track the wall had completely disappeared as had the scorched grass she was standing on. Rather now her entire panorama was filled with the beautiful landscape she had only previously seen through the hole in the wall. With this came a deep sense of inner peace and her response seemed almost spiritual in intensity.

The Application of PSTEC Tools on Children Aged Between 7-11 Years Old

I have worked with children as young as 6 years old successfully with PSTEC, though it depends on the maturity and concentration span of each individual child. When my daughter was about 2 years old she watched a particular film and a section of it freaked her out a little bit. 4 years on, even though she was able to laugh at herself for being scared about this particular thing, she was quite easily able to freak herself out. Occasionally she would call downstairs to us because she was scared about this particular character.

I had already suggested she try a Click Track but she was resistant to using it. However, after numerous nights of being shouted upstairs to placate her, I said that I will only stay up if she is willing to do a Click Track. She reluctantly agreed and at the end of the track she was amazed to discover that the image in her mind no longer produced any fear. She repeatedly closed her eyes to try to bring it back, to no avail. From that point on if there is a recurring fear I will only agree to stay with her if she first does a Click Track and this nips most problems in the bud.

For a personal consultation visit: www.themindhealer.co.uk

When I worked in a primary school (children aged 7-11) it was very experimental as I had no idea what specific challenges would arise or if they would be able to concentrate for so long. I asked each of them if they had ever played a computer game (most had) and regardless of their answer said that this was like a really easy game which would help them feel better about whatever was bothering them.

With children of any age I always frame the first experience of a Click Track as a practice run through as this cuts down any performance anxiety to a minimum. I have found that children of all ages prefer to keep their eyes open, at least during the first track and so I let them choose what they would like to do. If an additional track is required though I suggest they try it with their eyes closed "as this often helps people concentrate". For the majority it works with eyes open or closed.

I also do the tapping alongside them so that they can copy me if they like. Although this takes away from the processing power required to carry out the procedure, it still seems to work and many are happy to do it themselves for the second round.

The idea of the client copying you can equally be employed by the elderly or anyone for that matter who struggles with tasks such as these. One drawback of them keeping their eyes open is that they may be more prone to looking around the room. This isn't always a big thing but if they start reading things on the wall, then they may forget to focus on the thing that is bothering them. For this reason I advise them to stare at a pencil I place on the table in front of them throughout the session.

For a personal consultation visit: www.themindhealer.co.uk

I tell them that if they forget to look at the pencil that I shall remind them each time they look away. Some of the children require reminders every 20 seconds or so, especially those suffering from ADHD. Patience is required and even though they might keep forgetting, it often still works anyway.

Children of this age group possess a model of reality which is very open to change. Even compared with the age group of 11-16, there is a noticeable reduction in complexity as a whole due to the malleability of their mind. Here are some examples of what can be quickly achieved.

Miss C - recurring nightmare (aged 7)

Miss C had a recurring dream every night about being all alone on top of a tall bridge. The image made her feel very distressed and she was sobbing at the thought of it in the session. This had been going on for about a year and it just so happens that her parents went through a very bad patch at around that time which involved lots of arguing and there was talk of separation.

They managed to resolve these differences and are now getting on well but despite this the ideas of "alone" and not feeling secure were highly charged. I explained that it could be that her mind was still worried about her parents arguing and that maybe this was showing in the form of nightmares. When she thought back to the memories of her parents arguing it was highly emotionally charged with upset and anxiety.

For a personal consultation visit: www.themindhealer.co.uk

I suspect running the Click Track on the content of the memory or dream would have both had the same impact but I opted to have her focus on the arguments. One Click Track left her feeling very relaxed and neither the memories nor dreams evoked any feelings any more. We ended with a PSTEC Positive on, "everything is going to be ok". We didn't have much time and so didn't run any PSTEC Positive statements on sleeping well. However I suspected this wouldn't be required anyway as I believed that removing what appeared to be the cause would also remove the symptom of nightmares.

After this one session she changed into a much happier girl and all nightmares ceased.

Mr B - anxiety reading in front of class (aged 9)

At these kinds of ages the change can be quite dramatic. Mr B suffered from anxiety and in particular had panic attacks if he had to read at the front of the class. We imagined this scenario whilst going through a Click Track which cleared all fear. Next we ran a PSTEC Positive statement about feeling calm and confident when talking in front of people, after which he felt great.

To my amazement I saw him again 3 weeks later and he had completely transformed. Not only was he much more confident in general but he had also successfully auditioned for the lead role in the school play. These kind of dramatic changes seem more commonplace within this age group and I can't help but imagine how profoundly techniques such as PSTEC could

For a personal consultation visit: www.themindhealer.co.uk

impact people's lives if applied at this tender young age, nationwide.

Miss G – self-hate and self-harming (aged 10)

A few years ago Miss G had been verbally bullied. The reason why bullying at this age can be so damaging is that their model of reality is still very malleable. She seemed a shell of a person and suffered greatly from anxiety, self-hate and rarely spoke to anyone. Digging deeper I am pretty sure she would have had the belief that "people are dangerous" and "I am not worthy". However I only had 20 minutes and so we ran a Click Track on the painful memories of being bullied.

One track was all it took and she transformed. The next time I saw her a few weeks later she was happy, bubbly and confident. This is a clear example of beliefs disappearing along with emotions during a Click Track. Many months later I was informed that the positive changes had remained intact.

Mr U - multiple trauma and unstable home life (aged 7)

Mr U had an unstable home life. He wasn't able to see his mother for various reasons which he was finding really upsetting. He was also being bullied and lost a grandparent recently which had hit him very badly. As a consequence of all of this, he was quick to anger. He also suffered from quite severe ADHD.

We worked through the Click Track on upset over not being able to see his mother as often as he'd like and this also knocked away all of the unresolved grief and bullying anger. Due to his ADHD

For a personal consultation visit: www.themindhealer.co.uk

I had to constantly remind him to look at the pen in front of him to prevent him from looking around and reading signs on the wall. Also he would occasionally forget and just begin making up his own drum beat with his hands but a quick reminder brought him back to the task at hand.

One month later a little upset had returned due to further complications with his mother which we cleared with a Click Track. Everything else had remained gone though and overall he was much happier and better able to deal with day to day life.

Summary

As can be seen there are many similarities in working with younger children compared to adults. Often the results are more dramatic and require less unpicking because time hasn't had the chance to embed certain ways of thinking/feeling.

There is a greater chance that they will require additional assistance initially during the Click Track process, such as keeping their eyes open and copying someone else to start with until they become more familiar with the process. I have found the "copying" way of doing this better than moving their hands for them as younger children are able to copy and it still requires a bit of attention which is good. Overall this doesn't seem to impact the power of the tracks noticeably. I think maturity and attention span are greater signifiers of whether a child will benefit from a technique like PSTEC and this framework rather than age

For a personal consultation visit: www.themindhealer.co.uk

alone. I am sure even some 4-5 year olds could benefit so long as they are up for it and able and willing to follow it along.

For a personal consultation visit: www.themindhealer.co.uk

Conclusion

I wrote this book for several reasons. It is a good way to record my current thinking and ideas on working with people with a variety of ailments. It is also a book which I feel would have helped me when coming across sticking points with clients. Through experimentation and lots of trial and error I hope that it may help others overcome potential stumbling blocks and give ideas which might otherwise not be considered.

Although there are chapters on how to deal with specific issues, I hope that you will see how the ways of utilising the tracks and strategies within the framework are applicable to an almost limitless variety of problems. As with my other books, I included a huge number of case studies, simply because if you are anything like me, it is easier studying real world, practical applications of ideas; especially so when things don't quite go to plan.

There are quite a few extreme case studies for two reasons. First of all they now form the bulk of my day to day work. Secondly they offer the best chance to observe what happens when things aren't quite so straightforward.

For a personal consultation visit: www.themindhealer.co.uk

As well as provide self-helpers and people already familiar with tools such as PSTEC useful information, I really do hope that therapists who focus on modalities such as Cognitive Behaviour Therapy can find use in the information within. Rather than seeing it as an alternative, I hope you can see how it is more of a tool and set of ideas which could help strengthen the powerful work you already do, as well as provide solutions for situations which might otherwise tricky.

I really do hope that you have obtained some usable ideas from my ramblings and I wish you all the best with it.

For a personal consultation visit: www.themindhealer.co.uk

Appendix 1 - A description of PSTEC and the tools that are referred to

Percussive Suggestion Technique (PSTEC) at its core is an audio track that was created to reduce problematic feelings, whether this is anxiety, upset, anger and so on. Imagine the listener has a fear of spiders which they want to get rid of. First of all they would imagine a scenario involving spiders to activate the problem emotional state. They must rate the feeling in terms of intensity on a scale of 0-10, with 10 being the most unpleasant and 0 feeling calm.

They must then try to keep hold of the bad feeling whilst following the instructions on the 10 minute audio track. Throughout the 10 minutes is a voice firing positive suggestions at the listener with the aim of calming them. Very clever language patterns are utilised to ensure as much of the suggestion is accepted as possible.

Simultaneously the client has to listen out for three noises. Depending on which noise she hears she must either tap with her right hand, left hand or both hands together. The intention behind this is two-fold. It is frequently used as a pattern interrupt in which the voice requests that the listener focus on the problem scenario but immediately after this there is a change in the tapping sequence. In other words the problem thought is activated but then immediately interrupted repeatedly.

Also certain hand taps are split second timed with certain key calming words. The intention behind this is to make use of classical conditioning (anchoring) so that the subject's brain begins to associate calming ideas with particular hand movements.

Regardless of your clients or your beliefs as to why or whether the technique actually will work, for most people it simply does work even if they strongly believe it won't.

The Emotion Neutraliser Tracks:

I have just been describing the emotion neutralising tracks. Very often after just a few listens, the emotion disappears leaving a person feeling calm. Even though these tracks aren't primarily designed for belief change, there is often a corresponding belief change after the track as things often seem very different with the emotion removed.

The tracks are the standard Click Tracks, The EEF's (Enhanced Effectiveness Files) and Click Track 2015. I often ease people into the process with one of the standard Click Tracks. If more work is required I use one of the much more powerful EEF's or

For a personal consultation visit: www.themindhealer.co.uk

Click Track 2015 tracks. As a general rule of thumb, if I can sense that a person needs to feel safe I tend to go for the Click Track 2015 tracks as soon as possible as there is an emphasis on safety embedded in the suggestions. Unless I say otherwise I tend to use the medium length Click Track 2015 which is around 10 minutes long. In the case studies described I don't always specify which emotion neutraliser track I have used unless it is specifically relevant. It depends on how easy the client finds the Click Tracks and how much time we have. If multiple Click Tracks are required I often chop and change which I use so they get the benefit of the differing suggestions on each of the tracks.

The Accelerators:

These also act as an emotion neutraliser but can also be used with a PSTEC Positive type statement and also to aid recall of relevant past memories. I predominantly use the tapping Accelerator in sessions rather than the relaxational Accelerator, which is longer and involves no tapping, with a greater emphasis on suggestion alone. In the case studies, unless I say otherwise, if I mention an Accelerator, assume I mean the tapping Accelerator.

For a personal consultation visit: www.themindhealer.co.uk

The Belief Changers:

These include PSTEC Positive, PSTEC Negative and the Belief Blaster.

PSTEC Positive is used to create new beliefs and behaviours. I also describe ways it can be used to modify concepts and embed reframes which is explored more fully as you go through the book. In the case studies, whenever I mention use of PSTEC Positive, it is almost always the tapping version of PSTEC Positive Extra Power. Standard PSTEC Positive also works very well but as a personal preference, assume I mean the Extra Power tapping version.

PSTEC Negative is used to remove and de-charge problematic beliefs. I also describe how I use it to undo disempowering metaphors and concepts within a person's model of reality. I include how I use it to remove subconscious resistance.

The Belief Blasters are very new at the time of writing and do the same job as PSTEC Negative, albeit the tracks are structured very differently with no tapping involved. The instructions are more straightforward so I suspect people will find it easier to use as a whole. So far I have found it equally, if not more effective, than PSTEC Negative. The bulk of this work when it comes to undoing beliefs, will be focused on PSTEC Negative, so assume this whenever removing a belief is mentioned unless it is stated otherwise.

For a personal consultation visit: www.themindhealer.co.uk

I often use the belief change tracks once problem beliefs have been identified and better ones identified. Rather than just challenge the old beliefs these tracks make the changes at a more deep and lasting level.

Cascade Release

The Cascade Release Tracks can be used on emotions/problems for which there is no obvious cause. For example, imagine you feel a lot of anger but aren't sure why, you would focus on the anger rather than any causal memory and follow the instructions. This can be a very powerful tool when used at the right time. I shall be outlining my specific use of this along with tips and tricks I have worked out along the way. Along with PSTEC Negative, this is another track which can remove subconscious resistance when detected.

Appendix 2 - Winning Over Children with Behavioural Difficulties

When a private client comes to see me, they clearly want help and have often specifically sought me out to help them after reading one of my books, listening to one of my interviews or being recommended by someone else. This is a nice place to start for any presenting issue and as such my pre-talk is focused on getting them in the right frame of mind for understanding how our brains/thoughts/feelings work, as per the information at the beginning of this book.

I work in many schools which house children whose behaviour is too extreme for mainstream school. Many of them have been the victims of domestic violence, sexual abuse/exploitation and neglect with very unstable home lives. As a result they are carrying a lot of intense anger and upset around with them.

By the time they see me they have often seen numerous mental health professionals, they trust no-one and often have a lot of bravado and so even if they wanted help it is important to them not to be seen accessing help by their peers.

For a personal consultation visit: www.themindhealer.co.uk

This presents a unique set of challenges from getting them to agree to see me to start with, right through to having them trust me enough to open up to me and begin work. It took a lot of trial and error with different approaches but I am often now able gain their trust and have them be completely open with me after just a few minutes in most cases.

Any mention of therapy or counselling will immediately put them off. Therefore I have the staff at those type of schools tell the children absolutely nothing about me, other than that I would like to introduce myself for a few minutes after which they can go back to class. Getting out of class for a few minutes is something most of them are happy with. Also, they know that they don't have to say or do anything other than listen for a few minutes. This combination of facts helps to keep their inner "guards" well and truly relaxed at this point and they are happy to go along with proceedings.

Although I don't perform much these day, I am a psychological magician. Psychological magic involves intricately guiding a person's perception in the direction required for the apparent miracles to occur. Every single word and gesture is carefully thought out and scripted for this to occur. In a sense this is exactly what I am doing in my work, albeit the end result will be cooperation and trust rather than magic.

I begin explaining who I am and give a mini pre-talk. During this pre-talk my aim is to bypass all resistance and make them feel that I really know what I am talking about and that I can be trusted. It is also important that they see me as different to any other mental health professional they have worked with to reduce potential for resistance in that area.

"My name is Peter and I work with lots of the children and staff here at this school. I have certain tools and techniques which make it very easy to get rid of any anger, upset and anxiety without me having to know a thing. A lot of my work outside of schools is with soldiers who have seen horrors on the battlefield. At the time they get on with the job at hand but for many, even years on they can have flashbacks, panic attacks, their stomach can be constantly churning or they may have tightness in the chest.

Without telling me a thing we can very often clear all of this within 10 minutes or so. Afterwards they feel much calmer and happier and when they think back to what has happened, it almost feels as though it happened to someone else."

As you can see, I keep things very vague to avoid being pigeonholed by them. I also make some big claims and they will now be aware that if we do move forward they do not have to tell me a thing. Knowing this can be a big thing for many of these children and will help keep their guards from twitching. I don't work extensively with the army by any stretch of the imagination but I have worked with many soldiers privately.

The reason I focus on the army early on in the conversation, is because many of these children have respect for soldiers and even want to join the army after school. Also, many have a big tough image to keep intact but if they know soldiers are doing it,

For a personal consultation visit: www.themindhealer.co.uk

it allows them to keep the idea of their toughness intact. Another purpose it serves is to demonstrate the severity of trauma that these soldiers have been through, yet in a short space of time they can feel very different.

"Since being able to help so many soldiers, it occurred to me that I had suffered so much from anger and upset when I was at school due to various bad things that had happened and that these techniques would have made my life so much happier and easier. For this reason I have now focused on working in schools to help people who are suffering in the same way I did"

I suffered anxiety and depression a few years after school but I am aiming to gain as much rapport as possible and so a slight rewording of the emotions and when they occurred can help. I next ask if they become angry easier than they would like to. I focus on this emotion to start with because that is the most common problem emotion in this population. They nearly all say yes.

"You don't choose to feel angry though do you? It just happens all by itself right? We aren't born with anger but often things happen at different times in our lives during which our brain feels under attack. It therefore creates anger for survival reasons and you really do need it in certain circumstances don't you? For example, if someone has been bullied quite badly or has witnessed or experienced a lot of violence at home, it makes perfect sense for the brain to create anger. However, what often happens is that years then pass following these traumas and the brain doesn't readjust to the new reality, it just keeps the

For a personal consultation visit: www.themindhealer.co.uk

background anger high. Because of this you might find yourself kicking off at things which seem relatively minor.

For example if a teacher tells you off or someone looks at you in the wrong way you might feel the anger. However those things are just the trigger, the thing sitting on top of all the anger that is already there and it is that that is causing the problem".

This section takes away blame and gives them an explanation of their anger which they likely wouldn't have heard before and often makes complete sense to them for the first time. In other words it conveys more useful information whilst keeping their guards happy and receptive.

I then go on to describe the example I gave earlier in the book in which a 14 year old boy had severe anger issues but it turned out that it all stemmed from his when his father was violent towards him and his mother 10 years previously. I mention that he had no idea that he was still carrying rage from this event and that initially he was reluctant to remove the anger. I then remove potential resistance by explaining it has nothing to do with forgiveness and that they can retain whatever thoughts they have about the person/event in question. Also I make it clear that if anger is needed in day to day life that it will still become active. It will just be far less likely to activate when it isn't really necessary.

I explain how for another person who was very angry, it turned out that the cause was when his grandfather died many years ago and the pain was still raw. Anger and upset are often two sides of the same coin, with anger often sitting on top of upset as a way

For a personal consultation visit: www.themindhealer.co.uk

to deal with the pain. During this, I bypass resistance to removing grief by explaining that it is just a case of letting off some of the steam.

I ask if they would like to be less angry and the majority agree that their life would be better if this was the case. I next ask if they were angry at different ages until I pinpoint a rough time period at which it began. Once we have an approximate time we check to see if any of the following occurred at around that time:

- Death of a loved one
- Parental separation
- Bullying
- Domestic Violence
- Any health scares for self or others
- Any other reason which they prefer not to vocalise

If they have not experienced any of the above, I will ask them how they would wind themselves up if they had to. This can reveal certain scenarios or specific people and we can go down that route. By this time though, I literally have them in the palm of my hand and very often children who have never opened up to anyone tell me everything.

Everything that I have said to them is probably quite different to what they might typically expect from a counsellor and they are becoming aware of why they are thinking, feeling and behaving as they are. Possibly for the first time as well, they have a valid reason as to why it isn't under their complete control. Most of this pre-talk actually prevented them from talking whilst I

For a personal consultation visit: www.themindhealer.co.uk

systematically won their guards over and entered their castle. I also suggest indirectly through stories and information that, without them saying a word, I can make a dramatic change to how they are feeling in a matter of minutes.

Contrast this with more typical approaches, in which listening is the main starting point, at least initially. Everyone is different and I think it is essential for a therapist to be able to think on their feet and create an approach based upon the client sat in front of them. This is an extreme example but shows what can be achieved with some thought.

Once we have identified something to target, I say, "Imagine if I could just click my fingers like that and that churning in your stomach would be gone. Would that be a good thing?" I then explain there is a little more to it than that and explain the instructions of a Click Track and get right into it.

In these schools, there is a lot of bravado and they might be prone to winding each other up if they are seen to seek help. To reduce the risk of this making an impact, I reframe it before it happens. I explain that I have literally worked with pretty much everyone in the school and most people have really benefitted from it. I then go on to say that it is likely that a few people may try to persuade them not to bother or tease them for coming to see me. I say that most of these people who try to do the teasing have been to see me many times secretly and that it is just a front. I also dissuade them from doing the same thing to others as we go forward. This is a very useful and critical feature of

For a personal consultation visit: www.themindhealer.co.uk

working in these schools. Many of the children are like sheep and will follow what they think the crowd is doing.

If a few people decline to see me in front of others, it can very quickly and easily be seen as the new social norm. The above reduces the risk of that but I also request that these schools change their policy and that rather than determining who wants or needs to see me in form time in front of everyone else, rather they say nothing and I have mini chats with specific pupils in the corridor at break or just before form time, during which I ask if they would like to come for a chat later. Doing this again minimises their guards from interfering with the process before it has even begun and keeps the presence of their peers from interfering with their response.

Over time it can then result in it being the new norm to see me and a cool thing to do. As you can see I am taking control of perceptions and norms. I am also analysing and testing exactly what to say and how to say it to bring about the maximum chance of compliance. In every setting I work in, I am constantly refining and analysing what gets the best results and this is a clear example of it working. I remember the first time I entered a class in one of these schools to see if any the pupils wanted to speak to me. Unfortunately, I was wearing a pinkish shirt at the time so my sexuality was called into question by one of the pupils and it was a major battle to get any of them willing to see me.

Fast forward a few weeks and I had a fully formed slick formula which not only gets them to see me but also to open up very quickly, go through the session and minimises the risk they will

For a personal consultation visit: www.themindhealer.co.uk

discourage others from receiving help. Often the staff are amazed that a child who is so untrusting has been happy to open up to me so much after barely knowing me.

For a personal consultation visit: www.themindhealer.co.uk

Appendix 3 - Suggested Materials for PSTEC

I highly recommend all of Tim Phizackerley's work which can be found at http://pstec.org

In particular the following is essential for those wanting to delve further in the PSTEC Suite of Tools

PSTEC Level One

PSTEC Advanced

PSTEC Positive Secrets

I have written/recorded an audio book called "PSTEC in the Trenches", which gives very practical information on using the PSTEC Suite of Tools with my usual plethora of case studies.

I co-authored "PSTEC Advanced Part 2: Mapping Your Model of Reality" with Tim Phizackerley. In that piece of work I delve deep into the model of reality idea and demonstrate the power of using "characters" to personify our inner thoughts and thereby give us more self-awareness and control over them.

For a personal consultation visit: www.themindhealer.co.uk

For a personal consultation visit: www.themindhealer.co.uk

35373471R00180

Printed in Great Britain
by Amazon